W9-DGU-704

BATMAN & ROBIN

DARK KNIGHT VS. WHITE KNIGHT

BATMAN & ROBIN
DARK KNIGHT vs. WHITE KNIGHT

THE SUM OF HER PARTS

paul cornell
writer

scott mcdaniel
with *christopher jones*
pencillers

rob hunter
with *art thibert*
andy owens
inkers

TREE OF BLOOD

peter j. tomasi
writer

patrick gleason
penciller

mick gray
with *keith champagne*
tom nguyen
inkers

patrick brosseau
letterer

alex sinclair
guy major
artur fujita
colorists

patrick gleason
mick gray
with *alex sinclair*
cover artists

THE STREETS RUN RED

judd winick
writer

guillem march
andrei bressan
greg tocchini
with *andy smith*
artists

batman created by **bob kane**

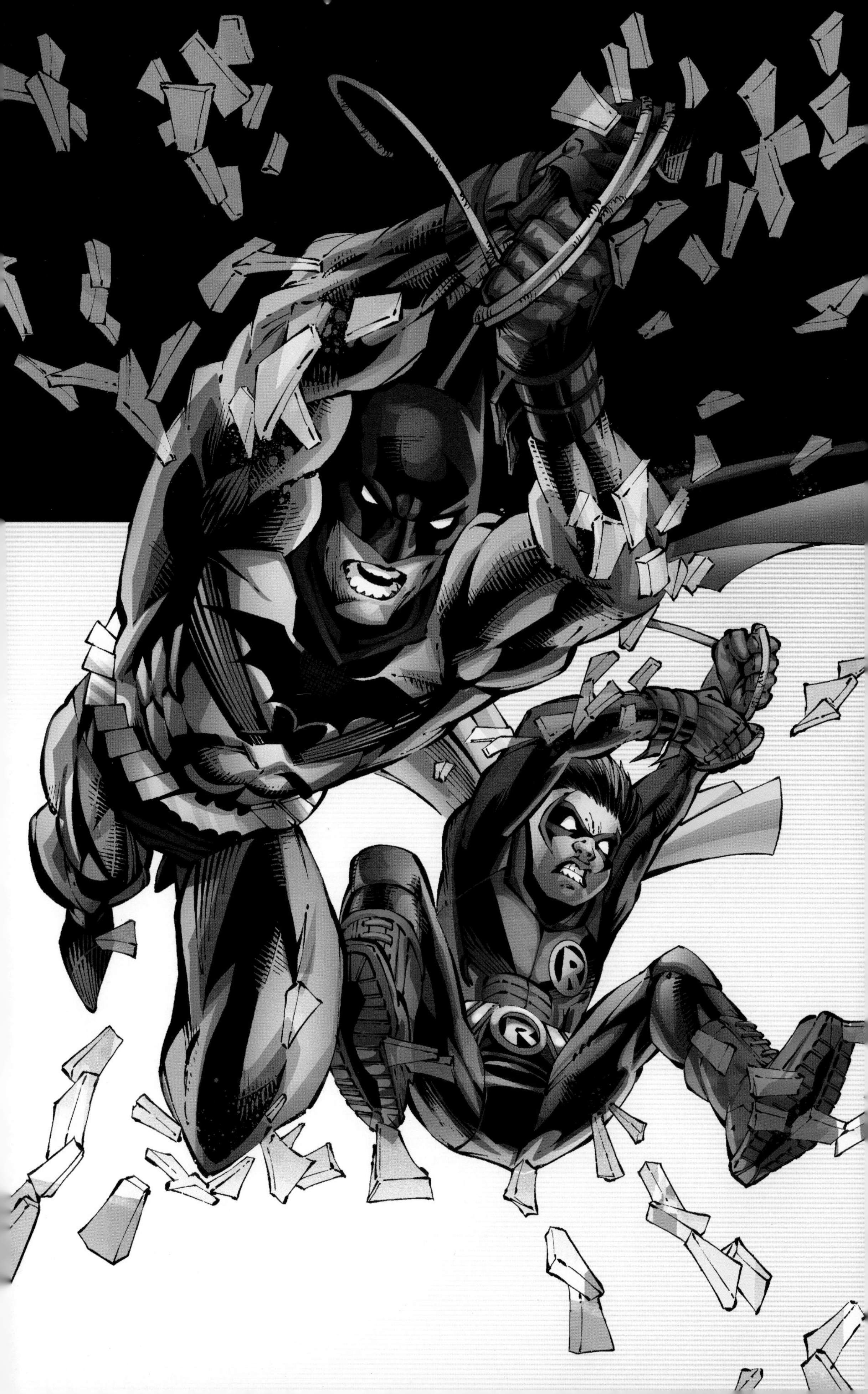

MIKE MARTS Editor – Original Series
JANELLE ASSELIN HARVEY RICHARDS Associate Editors – Original Series
KATIE KUBERT Assistant Editor – Original Series
IAN SATTLER Director – Editorial, Special Projects and Archival Editions
ROBBIN BROSTERMAN Design Director – Books
PETER HAMBOUSSI Editor
CURTIS KING JR. Publication Design

EDDIE BERGANZA Executive Editor
BOB HARRAS VP – Editor-in-Chief

DIANE NELSON President
DAN DIDIO and JIM LEE Co-Publishers
GEOFF JOHNS Chief Creative Officer
JOHN ROOD Executive VP – Sales, Marketing and Business Development
AMY GENKINS Senior VP – Business and Legal Affairs
NAIRI GARDINER Senior VP – Finance
JEFF BOISON VP – Publishing Operations
MARK CHIARELLO VP – Art Direction and Design
JOHN CUNNINGHAM VP – Marketing
TERRI CUNNINGHAM VP – Talent Relations and Services
ALISON GILL Senior VP – Manufacturing and Operations
DAVID HYDE VP – Publicity
HANK KANALZ Senior VP – Digital
JAY KOGAN VP – Business and Legal Affairs, Publishing
JACK MAHAN VP – Business Affairs, Talent
NICK NAPOLITANO VP – Manufacturing Administration
SUE POHJA VP – Book Sales
COURTNEY SIMMONS Senior VP – Publicity
BOB WAYNE Senior VP – Sales

BATMAN AND ROBIN: DARK KNIGHT VS. WHITE KNIGHT

DC COMICS 1700 Broadway, New York, NY 10019
A Warner Bros. Entertainment Company

Printed by RR Donnelley, Salem, VA, USA.
12/23/11. First Printing.

HC ISBN: 978-1-4012-3373-0
SC ISBN: 978-1-4012-3539-0

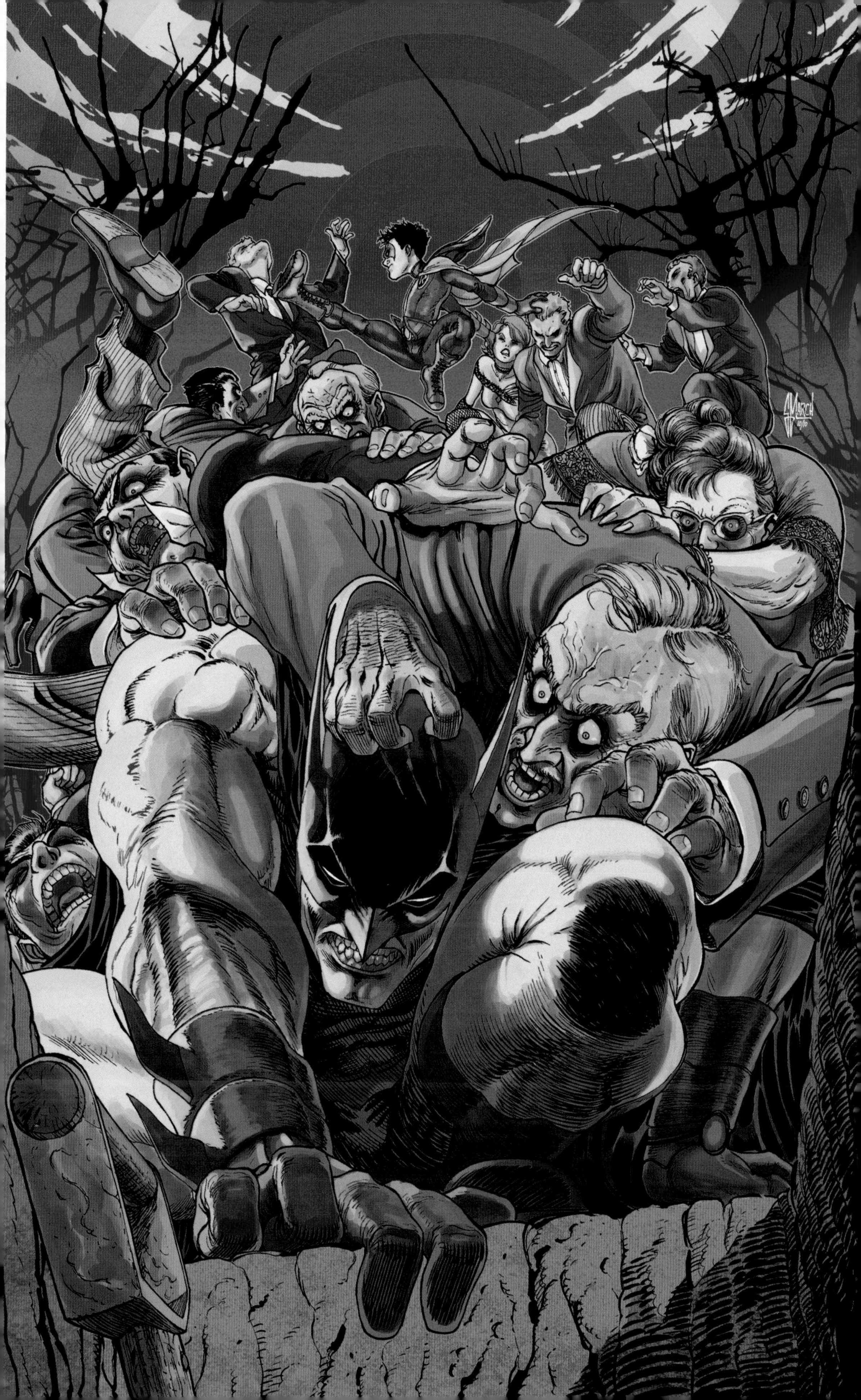

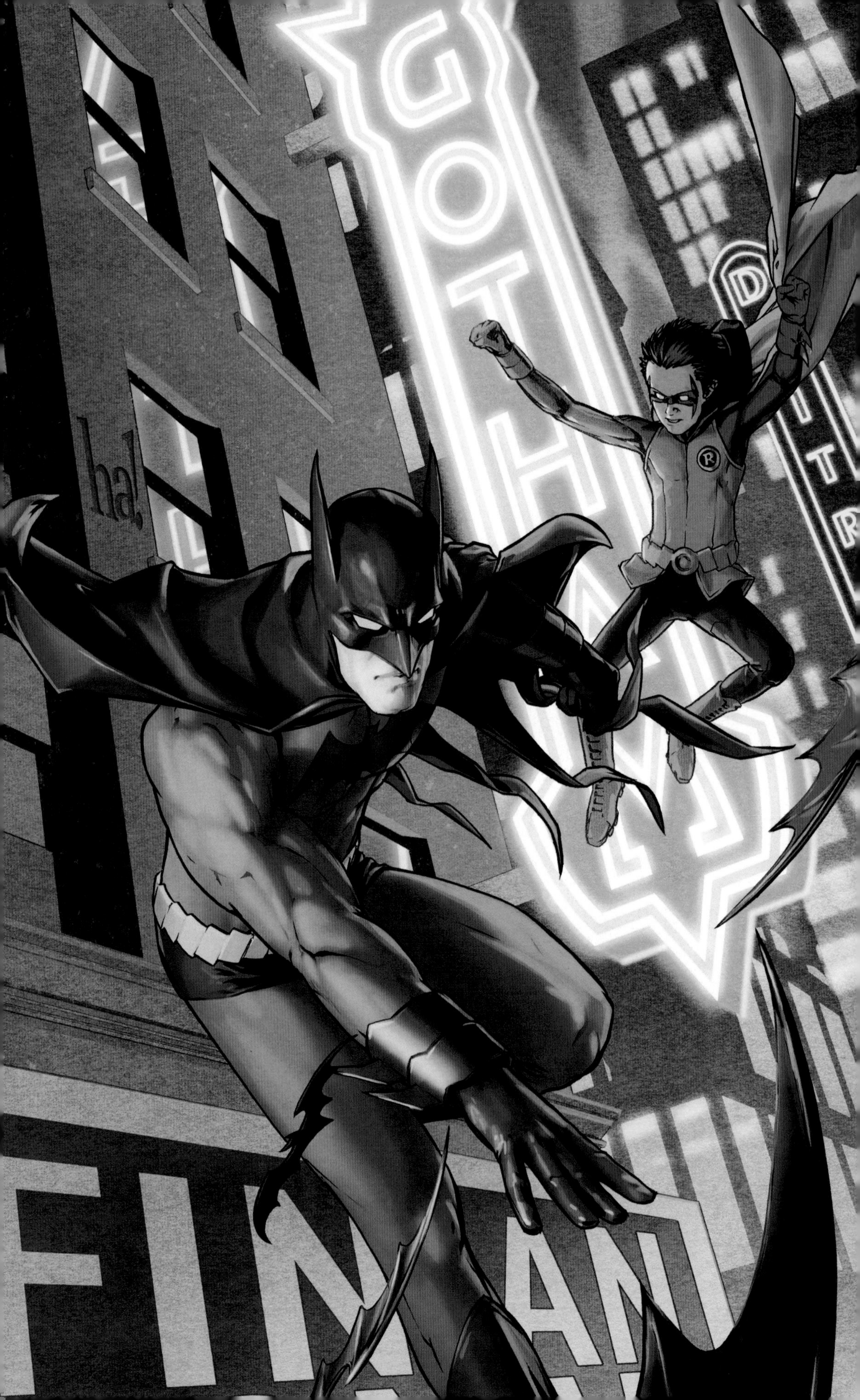
ha!

WHAT ARE WE MISSING?!

WHAT... ARE... WE... MISSING?!

WHAT ARE WE MISSING?!

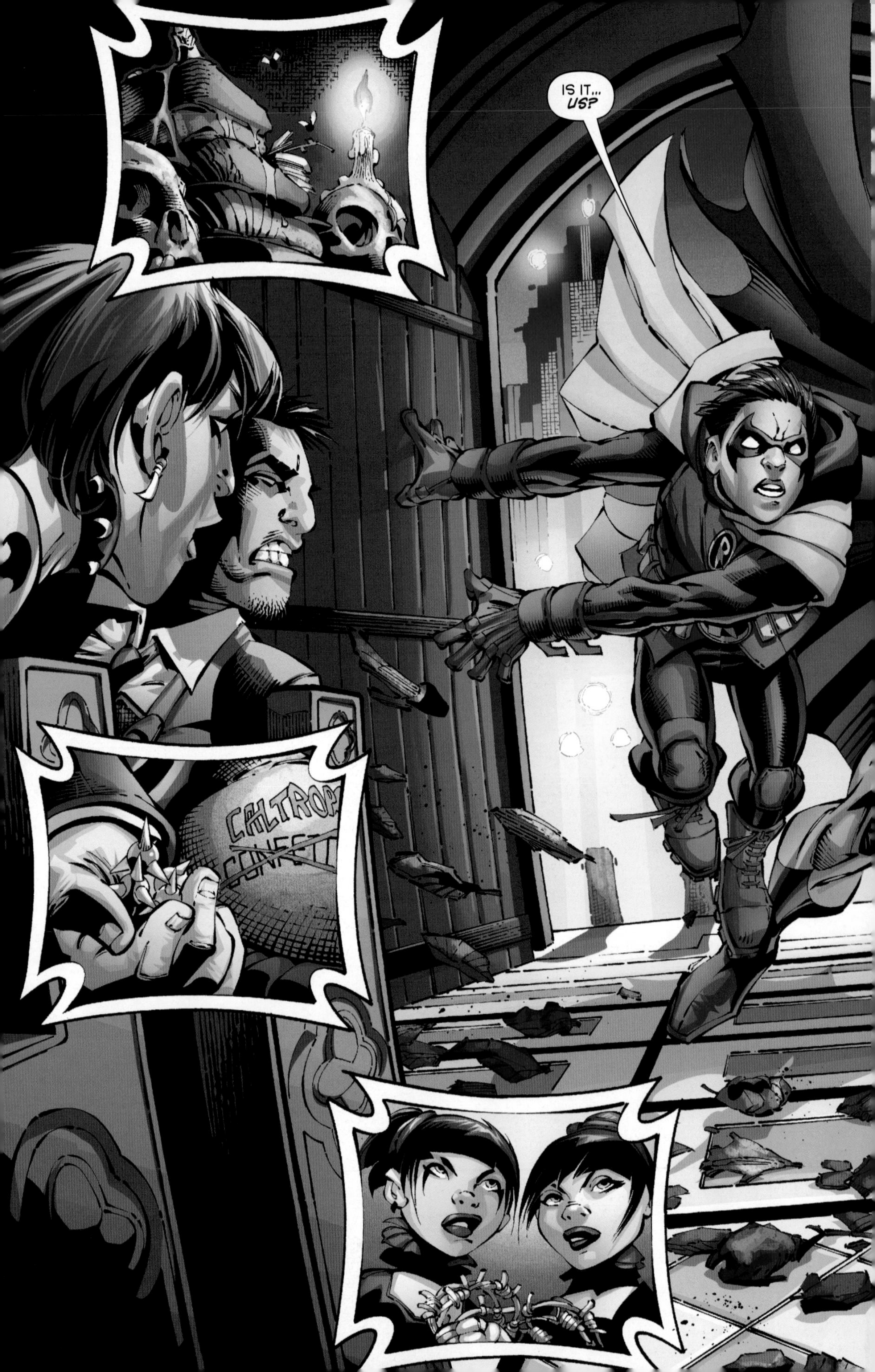
IS IT... US?
CALTROPS
CONFETTI

STOP THE WEDDING!

BATMAN AND ROBIN IN

THE SUM OF HER PARTS

PART 1 OF 3

PAUL CORNELL writer   SCOTT McDANIEL penciller   ROB HUNTER inker

ALEX SINCLAIR colorist   PATRICK BROSSEAU letterer   Covers by GUILLEM MARCH & GENE HA

ALL RIGHT. WE *BOTH* DID IT.

BUT WE SHOULD TRY *NOT* TO.

WHAT?

-tt-

WE BOTH HAD A *LINE.*

WELL, I'VE ALWAYS *WANTED* TO STOP A WEDDING.

I'M *SAYING*--

--WHAT WE DO--

--ISN'T MEANT TO BE--

--FUN!

NO, IT'S *NOT.*

BUT THAT DOESN'T MEAN WE CAN'T *HAVE* FUN DOING IT.

THAT'S AN ATTITUDE--

--YOU DIDN'T HAVE WHEN IT WAS JUST *YOU.*

CONSIDER: HASN'T THE FORMATION OF *BATMAN, INCORPORATED*--

--THE RETURN OF THE *ORIGINAL*--

--GIVEN EVERYONE LICENSE TO BE THEIR *OWN* SORT OF BATMAN?

IN YOUR CASE, WORRYINGLY *JOLLY* BATMAN?

HEH.

GOOD POINT--BUT *NO.*

ON THREE YOU DROP SMOKE AND STUN GAS--

"--AND I'LL DO FIVE MINUTES OF STAND-UP ON THE DIFFERENCES BETWEEN MEN AND WOMEN."

THREE NIGHTS PREVIOUSLY...

UNA NEMO

UNA NEMO, A FORMER GIRLFRIEND OF YOUR BOSS, BRUCE WAYNE...

...IF YOU BELIEVE THE MEDIA ABOUT HIS BEING YOUR BOSS, THAT IS.

THAT PART IS TRUE, COMMISSIONER.

MR. WAYNE'S CURRENTLY IN JAPAN, OR I'M SURE HE'D BE HERE.

IT LOOKS LIKE THE BODY WAS DUG UP IN A FRENZY...

BUT THEN CAREFULLY TAKEN AWAY.

AND THE SURROUNDING AREA IS EXTRAORDINARILY LACKING IN EVIDENCE.

WHAT WERE THE CIRCUMSTANCES OF MISS NEMO'S DEATH?

SIX WEEKS AGO.

A YACHT PARTY ON THE GOTHAM RIVER...

"...A JEWEL ROBBERY. FIRST-TIMERS.

"WE CAUGHT THEM THE SAME NIGHT.

"BY ALL ACCOUNTS, UNA NEMO WAS FORMIDABLE.

"I GUESS SHE PANICKED THE THIEVES."

BLAM!

"THE BODY WAS FOUND A COUPLE OF WEEKS LATER."

"THE POLLUTION HAD MADE A MESS OF IT."

SHE AND WAYNE HAD OFTEN BEEN SEEN ON THE TOWN.

BUT THAT HAD STOPPED A FEW WEEKS BEFORE HER DEATH.

WE USUALLY WOULDN'T PAY MUCH ATTENTION TO GRAVE ROBBING, BUT THE WAYNE CONNECTION...

IF SOMEONE IS TRYING TO HURT HIM...

WAIT, THIS IS CENTRAL CALLING.

WELL, IT GETS WILDER--

SOMEONE *RETURNED* THE BODY?

TO POLICE HEADQUARTERS. *KIND* OF THEM.

SECURITY CAMERAS?

"NO CHANCE OF IDENTIFICATION. GONE IN SECONDS."

ERGO: A *PLAYER*, MAYBE A *META*.

SENDING A MESSAGE.

SO WHAT'S THE CONTENT?

THE RING FINGER OF THE LEFT HAND HAS BEEN REMOVED, *RECENTLY*.

SOIL TRACES AND DECAY SAY THAT'S THE BODY FROM THE GRAVE. *BUT*, AND I'D BET MY PENSION ON THIS--

--IT'S *NOT* THE BODY OF UNA NEMO!

THE BATBUNKER

I'M TRULY *ASTONISHED*, SIRS--

--THAT NO ONE HAS CONTACTED MASTER BRUCE YET. HE WAS QUITE FOND OF MS. NEMO.

I WAS WAITING FOR *HIM* TO TAKE CARE OF IT.

I... WELL...

PROBLEMS, SIR?

I GUESS I WAS HOPING TO SOLVE THIS BEFORE HE HEARD. TO SPARE HIM, I GUESS.

HER DEATH HAPPENED WHILE HE WAS...AWAY. BUT I KNOW HE'D STILL FEEL RESPONSIBLE.

ALFRED, DID YOU EVER *MEET* MS. NEMO?

NO, SIR...

...THERE WERE YOUNG LADIES MASTER BRUCE BROUGHT *HOME*...

...AND THERE WERE YOUNG LADIES HE DID *NOT.*

"SOMETIMES HE FELT HE COULD BE A REAL PERSON, ALLOWING HIMSELF TO LOVE AND BE LOVED...

"...AND SOMETIMES HE FELT THAT 'BRUCE WAYNE' WAS A...COVER STORY...WHICH REQUIRED THE PRESENCE OF 'GIRLS.'

"NEEDLESS TO SAY...

"...HE WAS AS CAREFUL TO DO NO HARM IN THAT ASPECT OF HIS LIFE--

"--AS IN ALL OTHERS.

"NOW, I CAN ONLY HOPE--"

--THAT THIS LATEST RECOGNITION THAT HE HAS FRIENDS AND *ALLIES*--

--LEADS HIM ONCE MORE TO THE *FORMER* LIFESTYLE.

ACCORDING TO THE WITNESSES, NEMO WAS SHOT THROUGH THE *FOREHEAD* AT POINT BLANK RANGE.

TWO JANE DOES ARE FISHED FROM THE RIVER EVERY WEEK. WITH THAT TURNOVER, DAMAGE TO THE BODIES, KNOWING THE LABS, LET'S SET ASIDE MORGUE DUPLICITY.

FOR NOW.

THE PERP MIGHT BE SAYING THEY KNEW THAT WASN'T NEMO IN THE GRAVE--

--MAYBE TAUNTING THE POLICE ABOUT IT.

SHE WASN'T MARRIED. THE SLAB SHOTS OF JANE DOE DON'T SHOW A RING, EITHER.

SO WHY TAKE *THAT* FINGER?

EMAIL FROM THE COMMISSIONER--

I KNOW WHAT IT SAYS--

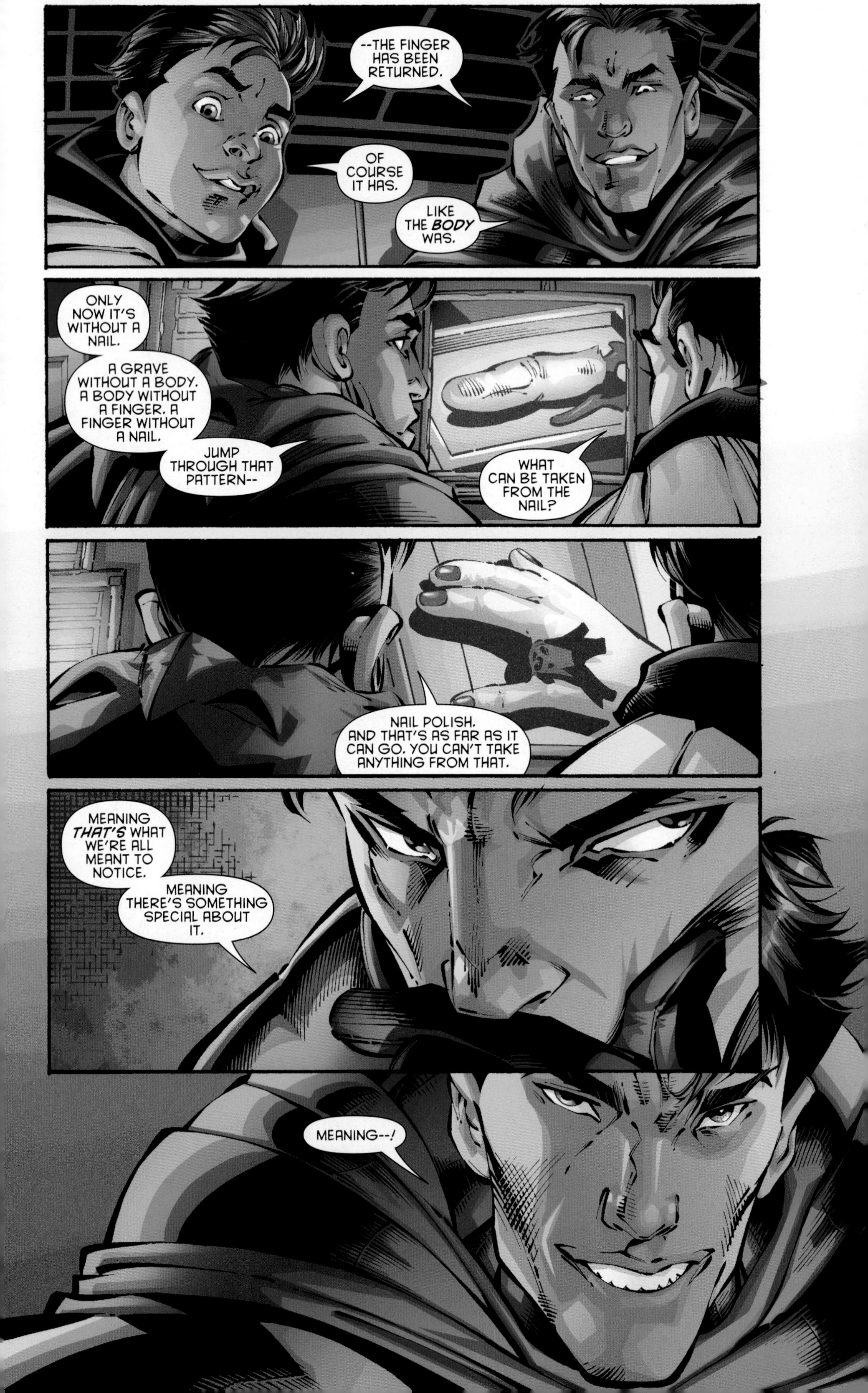
--THE FINGER HAS BEEN RETURNED.
OF COURSE IT HAS.
LIKE THE *BODY* WAS.
ONLY NOW IT'S WITHOUT A NAIL.
A GRAVE WITHOUT A BODY. A BODY WITHOUT A FINGER. A FINGER WITHOUT A NAIL.
JUMP THROUGH THAT PATTERN--
WHAT CAN BE TAKEN FROM THE NAIL?
NAIL POLISH. AND THAT'S AS FAR AS IT CAN GO. YOU CAN'T TAKE ANYTHING FROM THAT.
MEANING *THAT'S* WHAT WE'RE ALL MEANT TO NOTICE.
MEANING THERE'S SOMETHING SPECIAL ABOUT IT.
MEANING--!

WHAT IS--?

FLAMMM!

AHH!

HER...HER FINGERNAILS! THEY WERE--!

PAINTED WITH A DELAYED ACTION *EXPLOSIVE* MIXTURE.

THE SAME COLOR AS THE CORPSE'S ORIGINAL NAIL POLISH.

TO TAKE THE BODY AWAY FROM US.

I DOUBT WE'LL EVER FIND OUT WHO THIS JANE DOE WAS.

THE MESSAGE IS COMPLETE. THIS ONE TAKES THINGS AWAY.

SO WHAT THEY *LEAVE*--

--IS *DELIBERATE.*

CHEMISTS are EXPERT in BONDING

You are invited to a
Night Wedding.
Everything is ready.
But something is missing.
St. Peter's Church, Gotham.

SO--

HKSS!

YOU'RE A RETIRED CHEMICAL ENGINEER, SPECIALIZING IN FLAMMABLES. STILL DO IT AS A HOBBY. ADVERTISE YOUR SERVICES.

IN *THIS* TOWN?

I...I...I'M SORRY!

A VOICE ON THE PHONE HIRED ME--

WHAT SORT OF--?

A *DISGUISED* VOICE!

IT...LEFT THINGS OUT, A WORD EVERY SENTENCE!

CASH WAS LEFT. MY REACTIVE PAINT WAS COLLECTED.

BUT TONIGHT... A CROWD OF THESE... THESE...

BATMAN--

--THEY'RE SPRINGING THEIR *TRAP* NOW.

THEIR *TRAP?!*

WE *DELIBERATELY* WALKED INTO IT.

YOU HEAR WHAT THEY'RE CHANTING AGAIN?

WHAT... ARE... WE... MISSING?!

WHY...WHY ARE THEY *DOING THAT?!* WHY AREN'T YOU TRYING TO GET US *OUT* OF HERE?!

THE TRAIL ASKED US WHAT WAS MISSING.

WHAT'S MISSING HERE IS THE *BRIDE.*

BUT A BRIDE ARRIVING WOULD COMPLETE THIS PICTURE.

AND THAT'S NOT WHAT *YOU* DO--

--*IS* IT?!

AH. SHOULDN'T HAVE MENTIONED THE MISSING *WORDS.* TOO MUCH *DETAIL.*

THERE WAS A *REAL* CHEMIST. BUT *HE'S* MISSING NOW. YOU WON'T FIND HIM.

SO, NO *BRIDEGROOM...*

BUT--!

NO!

HOORAY!

HE'S VANISHED INTO THEM!

SEVERAL OF THEM WILL HAVE BEEN INJURED WHEN HE LANDED.

GENUINE *DEVOTION.*

METICULOUS. QUICK-WITTED. INSPIRING.

WHO *IS* THIS GENERAL?

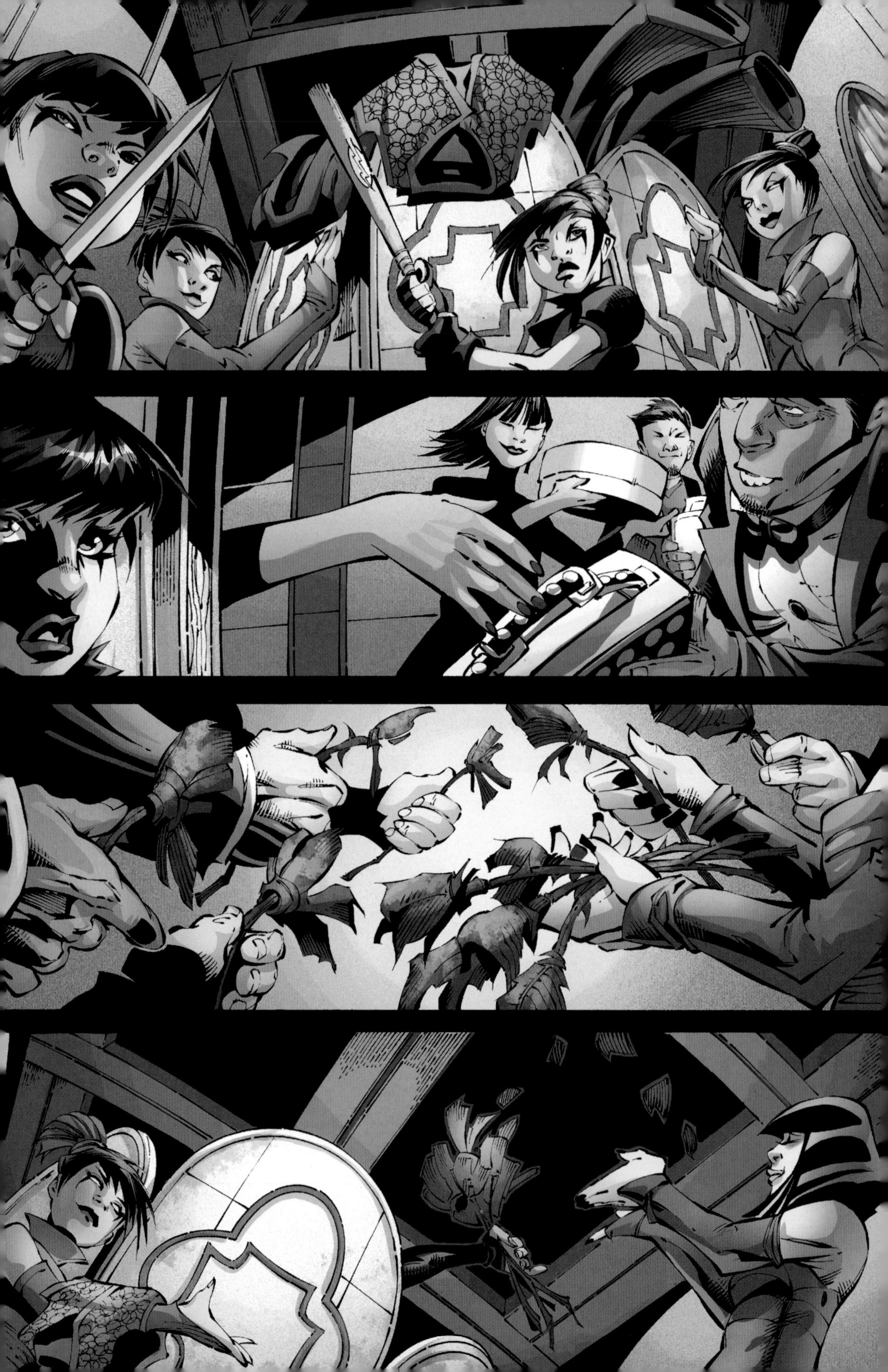

IF THIS WERE THE OLD DAYS I'D RAISE AN EYEBROW AND SAY "IT'S A WOMAN!"

AS IT STANDS--

--I'M JUST AMAZED SHE COULD FOOL ME ABOUT THAT EVEN FOR A MINUTE.

GOOD EVENING, BATMAN!

MY NAME IS THE ABSENCE!

THANK YOU FOR NOTICING ME!

FINALLY!

MY MAIDEN NAME WAS *UNA NEMO.*

AND *NOW YOU* CAN SEE--

--WHAT YOU'VE BEEN *MISSING!*

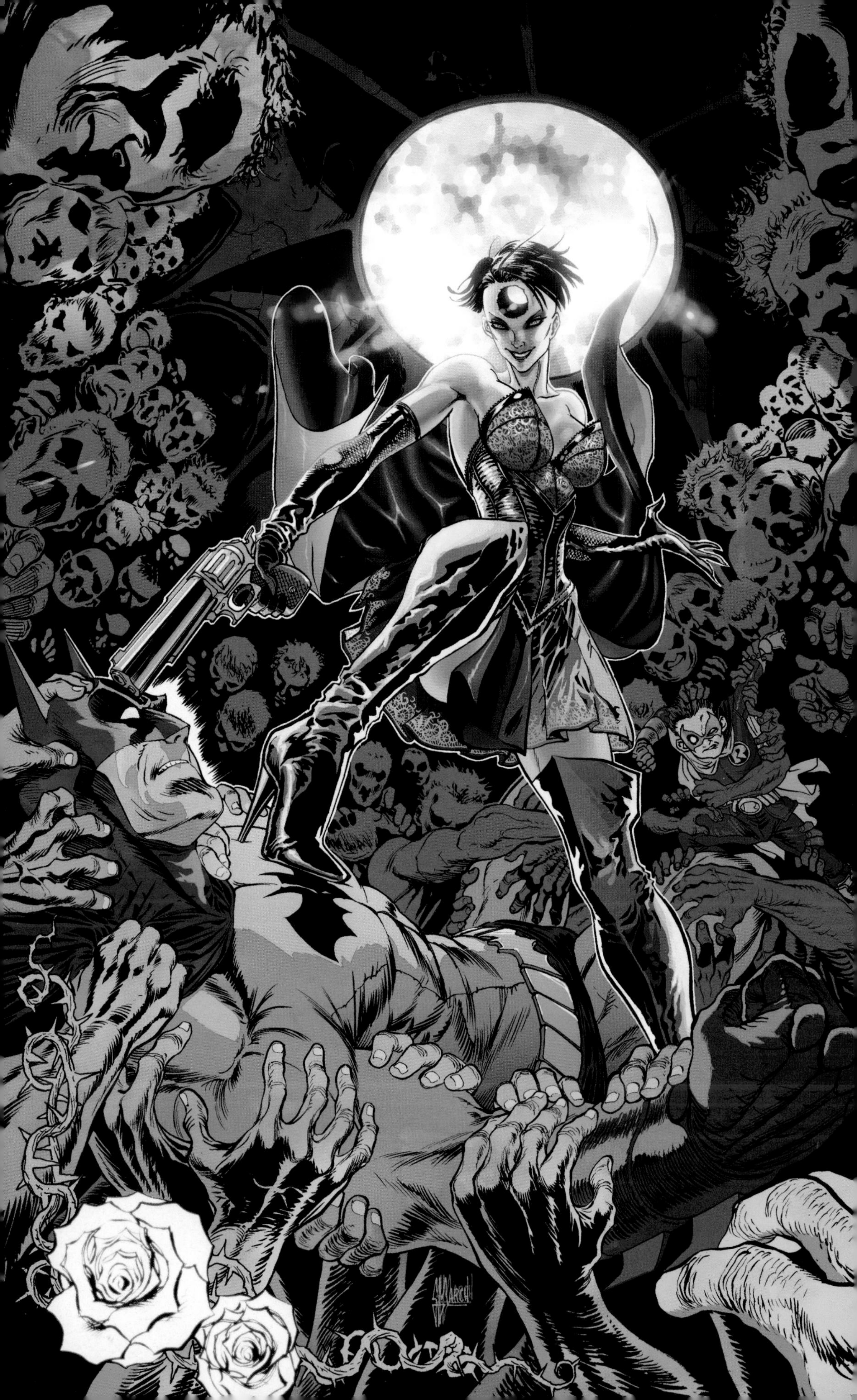

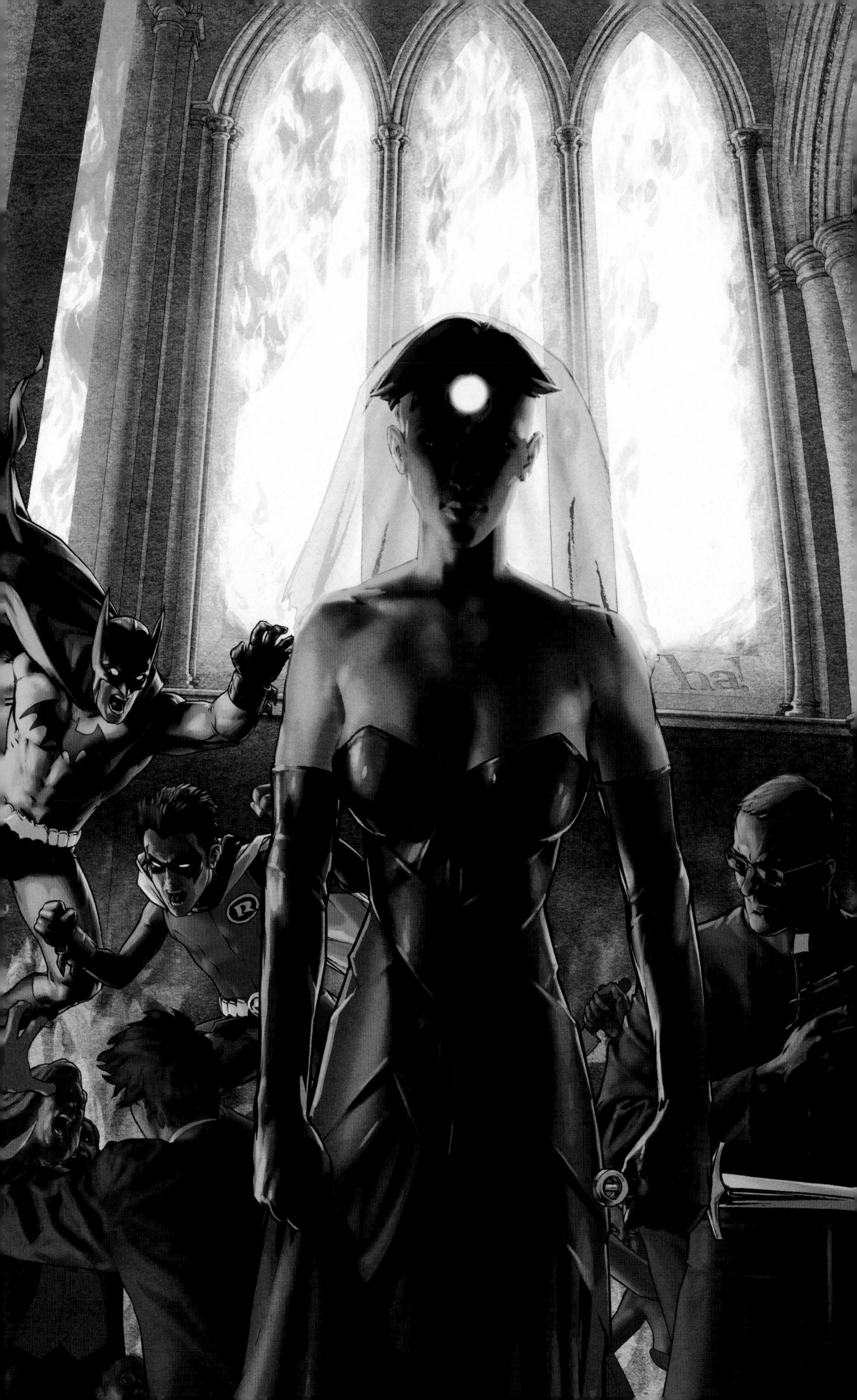
ha!

NO REPLY?

NOTHING?!

BATMAN AND ROBIN

IN

THE SUM OF HER PARTS PART 2 OF 3

PAUL CORNELL writer SCOTT McDANIEL with CHRISTOPHER JONES pencillers

BOB HUNTER, ART THIBERT and ANDY OWENS inkers GUY MAJOR colorist PATRICK BROSSEAU letterer

WE ENTERED YOUR TRAP *DELIBERATELY*, MISS NEMO.

WHICH WAS OBVIOUSLY SET BY A *LUNATIC*.

HAH. TRYING TO *PROVOKE* ME.

I *WILL* TALK AND TALK.

I *WILL* DO EXTREME THINGS--

--BUT NOT, I'M AFRAID, *UNPLANNED* ONES.

I WAS PROVOKED *LONG* AGO!

BRUCE WAYNE NOW SEEMS TO HAVE AN *ARMY* OF DETECTIVES--

--SO I CAN *LOSE* A FEW OF YOU--

--AND STILL GET MY *MESSAGE* DELIVERED!

FWA-BOOOM!

KEEP BATMAN AND ROBIN *CONSCIOUS.*

WE'VE A *LOT* TO GET THROUGH.

STOP STRUGGLING!

CONSIDER--

--BEING *HAMSTRUNG.*

PLENTY OF BATMEN TO TAKE YOUR PLACE, RIGHT?

BETTER. NOW--

--I *SAID* I WAS GOING TO TALK.

LET ME TELL YOU WHAT I'M *NOT*--

"--A FOOL."

SEVERAL MONTHS AGO...

SO, ERM, BRUCE...

...I'M AFRAID I JUST DON'T *GET* THIS.

THIS IS WHAT, OUR *SIXTH* DATE?

WE'VE TALKED ALL MANNER OF TRIVIA. WE'VE DANCED. WE'VE *FLIRTED*...

...BUT IT'S LIKE YOU'RE STILL KEEPING ME AT *ARM'S LENGTH.*

I'M WEALTHIER THAN *YOU,* I THINK.

BUT YOU TREAT ME LIKE A *GOLD-DIGGER.*

LIKE YOU'RE AFRAID OF ME HAVING YOU AT A DISADVANTAGE.

LIKE YOU'RE AFRAID OF ME *HAVING* YOU.

WHAT I'M SAYING IS--I'LL BE YOUR FRIEND BUT I WON'T BE A BEARD.

THIS IS OUR LAST "DATE"--

UNA, PLEASE, WAIT--

--I'VE... MISCALCULATED.

THIS WAS... HOW IT *HAD* TO BE.

IF YOU WANT TO STOP DOING THIS, I'LL UNDERSTAND.

BUT THERE *IS* A REASON--

--"AND ONE DAY, MAYBE YOU'LL UNDERSTAND."

THAT'S ALL HE SAID. AND NOW HE'S STOPPED SEEING ME, AND EVERYONE SAYS HE'S... "INDISPOSED."

AND YOU LEFT IT AT THAT?!

UNA, YOU RUN YOUR COMPANY LIKE A MAN, YOU'RE DISTANT LIKE A MAN, YOU'RE EMOTIONALLY DUMB LIKE A MAN!

I WAS ON BRUCE'S ARM FOR A WHILE. WE ONLY GOT SO FAR--

--AND NO FURTHER.

THAT'S ALWAYS THE BRUCE WAYNE STORY. AT LEAST WITH GIRLS LIKE US.

PEOPLE SAY BRUCE IS VERY PRINCIPLED.

"NOT BEFORE MARRIAGE." AND THAT WHAT HE'S LOOKING FOR--

--IS SOMEONE TO GET SERIOUS WITH.

TO PROPOSE TO.

THAT'S WHAT YOU WALKED AWAY FROM!

YOU THINK? AND, LISTEN, I'M NOT--

I KNOW! CROSS MY HEART AND--

ACKKHHH!

TERRI?!

BLAM! BLAM!

THIS ISN'T A HOSTAGE SITUATION--

--THIS IS A ROBBERY!

TERRI!

KK-KK-!

JEWELRY AND TECH IN THE SACKS NOW!

YOU-- YOU--

--NOTHING!

BLAM!

"I REMEMBER *NOTHING* OF WHAT HAPPENED NEXT...

"LITTLE NEMO IN SLUMBERLAND.

"UNTIL...

AH!

"WHY WAS I *ALIVE?*"

"HOW WAS I ALIVE?!"

WUH--?

"NOW I THINK THAT THE POLLUTION FROM THE RIVER DID SOMETHING TO THE WOUND."

MEDIA BILLIONAIRE SHOT DEAD

I...I HAVE TO GET HOME.

"A LONG, FROZEN WALK.

"TIME TO THINK.

"ABOUT WHAT I'D MISSED.

"MAYBE A PROPER FRIENDSHIP WITH TERRI?

"ABOUT A LOVING COMMITMENT FROM BRUCE?

"I WAS STILL IN SHOCK. I WAS STILL A FOOL."

HOME SECURITY CODE... AUTOMATIC ENTRY... NEMO...BLUE...

MS. NEMO IS HOME.

HOME SYSTEM, GET ME A SMART MEDIC PROGRAM.

"I'D NEVER HAD A HEAD X-RAY, NEVER KNOWN I HAD THESE CONDITIONS."

"THAT I WAS--"

DANDY WALKER SYNDROME.

AND THAT'S JUST THE BEGINNING OF IT...

"MY HEAD WAS EMPTY."

HYDROCEPHALY

FULLY FUNCTIONAL CONSCIOUS PROCESSES MAINTAINED BY THIN FILM OF GREY MATTER.

INJURY HAS LEFT YOU UNHARMED.

BUT MASSIVELY INCREASED FLOW OF OXYGEN TO BRAIN MAY HAVE UNKNOWN EFFECTS.

YES, I CAN FEEL THAT...DOING SOMETHING.

JUST TELL ME HOW TO LIMIT IT AND PREVENT INFECTION.

TONIGHT'S ATTACK *SEEMED* RANDOM...

...BUT UNTIL WE KNOW FOR SURE, LET THE AUTHORITIES THINK I'M DEAD. I DON'T WANT SOME BENT COP COMING TO FINISH THE JOB.

GOODNIGHT, HOME SYSTEM.

"I DISCOVERED I DIDN'T NEED TO *SLEEP*.

"A WEIRD SENSATION CREPT OVER ME--"

I'M *MISSING* SO MUCH.

I *WANT* SO MUCH.

MY OWN *FUNERAL?*

I'VE *ALWAYS* WANTED TO SEE *THAT!*

"I HAD NO FAMILY TO WORRY ABOUT...

"SO I DECIDED I WAS GOING TO ENJOY MY FUNERAL--

"--AND *THEN* TELL EVERYONE WHAT HAPPENED."

"BUT AT THE SERVICE, SEVERAL THINGS TOOK ME BY SURPRISE...

"...FIRSTLY, NOBODY WAS PARTICULARLY *UPSET.*

"I'D BEEN A PERFECTLY HONEST, EVEN *KIND,* BUSINESSPERSON.

"WERE THEY MISSING SOME EXTRA *WARMTH* THEY EXPECTED OF A WOMAN?

"I STARTED TO RELY ON THE THOUGHT THAT *BRUCE* MIGHT BE UPSET.

"THAT I'D *MISUNDERSTOOD* HIM, LIKE A MAN IN A GOTHIC ROMANCE.

"HE...HE DIDN'T EVEN *ATTEND.*

"I'D BEEN PLANNING TO THROW OFF MY HAT AND *SURPRISE* EVERYONE..."

"BUT IT OCCURRED TO ME...

"...THEY'D STOPPED MISSING ME SO QUICKLY...

"...SO IF I CAME BACK...

"...WOULD THEY BE *PLEASED?*

"WOULD THEY EVEN ACCEPT IT WAS *ME?*

"INCREASED OXYGEN FLOW TO THE BRAIN CAN *INCREASE INTELLIGENCE.*

"IT CAN MAKE ONE *THINK FASTER.*

"IT CAN MAKE ONE *UNDERSTAND--*"

AHHHH!

IT'S NOT MY FAULT.

IT'S *THEIR* FAULT.

MY NEEDS *CAN'T* BE SATISFIED--

--BY THEIR *APPROVAL.*

"YOU CAN'T UNDERSTAND INCREASED THINKING SPEED UNTIL YOU ACTUALLY *EXPERIENCE* IT.

"I USED MY SECRET ACCESS TO REMOVE MY FORTUNE FROM MY COMPANY.

"FROM THOSE WHO HADN'T *MISSED* ME.

"I'D IMMEDIATELY FIGURED OUT HOW *RANDOM* MY MURDER REALLY WAS...

"BUT STILL, WHEN BRUCE FOUNDED *BATMAN, INCORPORATED*--

"--I EXPECTED HIM TO *LOOK* INTO IT.

"HAVING STOLEN MY OWN MONEY, LEAVING SUBTLE CLUES BEHIND--

"--I EXPECTED *ONE* OF *SO MANY* DETECTIVES TO REALIZE I WAS *ALIVE.*"

HE HASN'T *NOTICED.* HE HASN'T MISSED *ME.*

SO I'LL *MAKE* HIM.

AND DO WHAT *ELSE* NEEDS TO BE DONE.

AH. I KNOW *HOW.*

IN *EVERY* DETAIL.

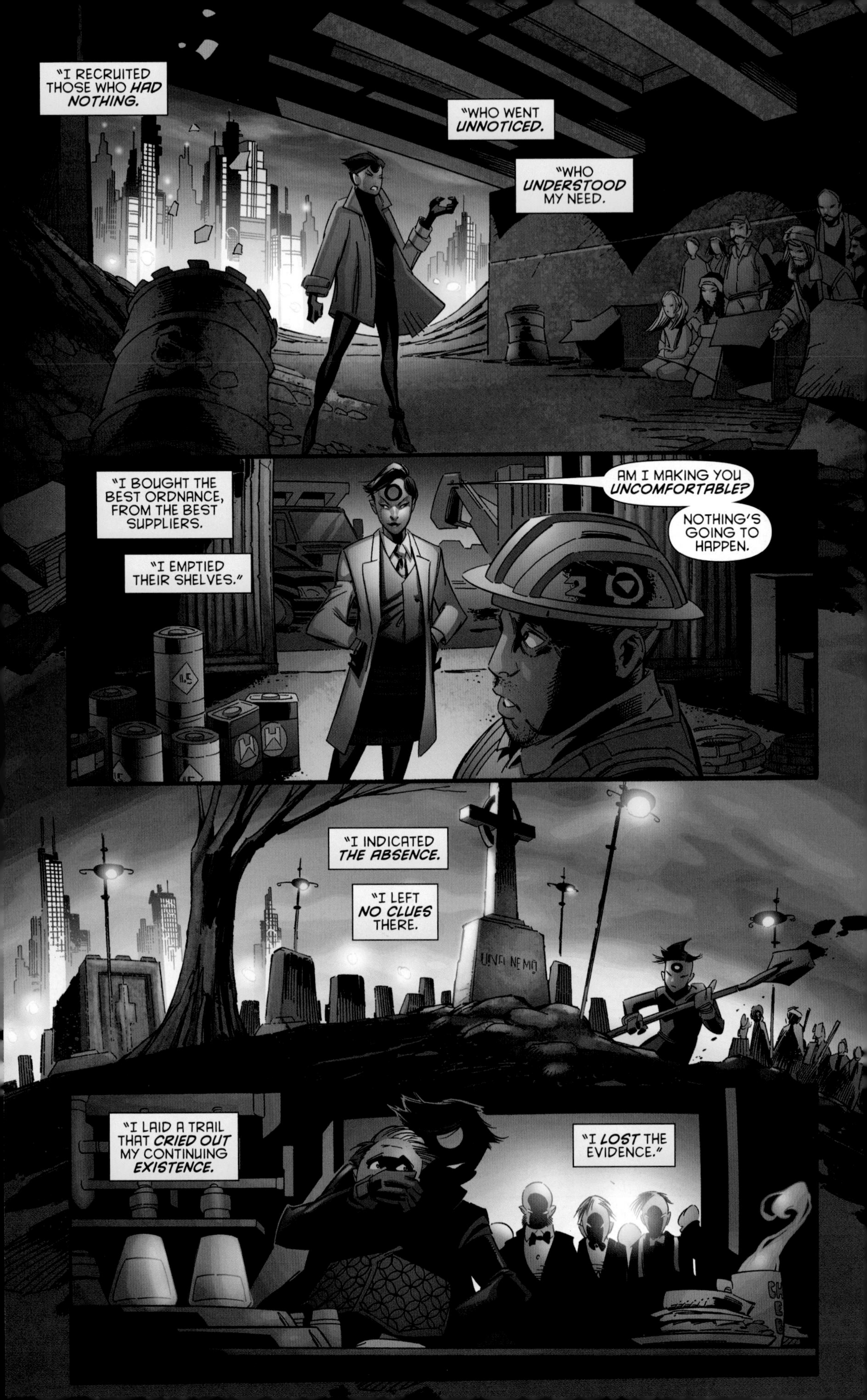
"I RECRUITED THOSE WHO *HAD NOTHING.*
"WHO WENT *UNNOTICED.*
"WHO *UNDERSTOOD* MY NEED.
"I BOUGHT THE BEST ORDNANCE, FROM THE BEST SUPPLIERS.
"I EMPTIED THEIR SHELVES."
AM I MAKING YOU *UNCOMFORTABLE?*
NOTHING'S GOING TO HAPPEN.
"I INDICATED *THE ABSENCE.*
"I LEFT *NO CLUES* THERE.
UNA NEMO
"I LAID A TRAIL THAT *CRIED OUT* MY CONTINUING *EXISTENCE.*
"I *LOST* THE EVIDENCE."

WELL, *NOTHING* WILL COME OF *NOTHING*.

HAVE I NOT MADE YOUR HEART GROW *FONDER*?

BRUCE WAYNE FUNDS MY OPERATIONS. I'VE *MET* THE MAN... I MAY *KNOW SOMETHING* ABOUT THIS.

AND... I THINK I CAN SEE WHAT *HAPPENED*.

YOU DON'T KNOW ALL THE *FACTS*--

FACTS?!

I'M MORE *INTELLIGENT* THAN YOU. I *FOOLED* YOU!

YOU DON'T GET TO "MANSPLAIN" TO *ME!*

THIS IS *RIDICULOUS.* WE'RE HERE BECAUSE OF *HER ERROR.*

ROBIN, WHEN I'M IN THIS *PARTICULAR* SITUATION--

COULD YOU *NOT* BE MR. DIPLOMATIC?!

NOT MUCH POINT PERSUADING ME, YOU KNOW...

...IT'S IN ONE EAR AND OUT THE OTHER.

SOME OF THESE FOLKS WOULD *LOVE* TO DIE FOR ME.

I FILL A *VOID* IN THEIR LIVES, AND VICE VERSA.

I'M SURE THAT WHILE THEY'LL TRY TO *HOLD* YOU HERE, AT LEAST *ONE* OF YOU WILL ESCAPE--

"--AND TELL BRUCE WAYNE WHAT HE WAS *MISSING!*"

BUT UNTIL HE NOTICES I'VE *GONE*--

--I'LL KEEP *REMINDING* HIM.

GLARRGGHHHHH!

GADGETS AND TRICKS CAN'T HELP US, ROBIN. WAIT UNTIL THE SMOKE...

...WEAKENS THEM...BEFORE US...

...AND... ON MY MARK...

GO!

NEED TO SAVE...

AS MANY OF *THEM*...

...AS POSSIBLE!

FWA-BOOOOMM!

TWO HOURS LATER... THE BATBUNKER.

IT'S RIDICULOUS, THE KNOTS PEOPLE GET INTO.

"DATING" CAN *DO* THAT?!

YOU'LL UNDERSTAND MORE WHEN YOU'RE OLDER, MASTER DAMIAN.

GIVEN MY UPBRINGING, PENNYWORTH--

--I *DOUBT* IT.

I'M GOING TO END UP JUST LIKE MY *FATHER.*

WHAT DOES *THAT* MEAN?

IT MEANS--

--WHO *PRETENDS* TO LIKE SOMEONE?

YOU'RE TALKING LIKE IT'S HIS FAULT. WE HAVE TO *PROTECT* BRUCE FROM--

DO WE, MASTER RICHARD?

I DON'T THINK THE *BATMAN* NEEDS MUCH IN THE WAY OF *PROTECTION*--

--DO YOU?

JAPAN.

WHAT?! THAT ALL HAPPENED WHILE... WHILE I WAS...*AWAY.* I HADN'T HEARD ABOUT--

--AND WITH TOMMY ELLIOT IMPERSONATING ME...HE DIDN'T--

--NO.

TELL HER I KNOW WHAT HAPPENED NOW.

THAT I'M... *DESPERATELY* SORRY.

I *HAVE* TO STAY HERE SEVERAL MORE DAYS AND THEN I'M OFF TO ARGENTINA, BUT...

...DICK, LISTEN...

...THINK IT THROUGH...

...I'M SURE YOU'RE COMING TO THE *SAME CONCLUSION* AS I AM...

WHAT SHE'LL DO *NEXT.*"

"CYCLOPEAN"? NO...

Get 2nd Source on JS

Call Marts Wed

·check gates ·recheck!

...THE CITY COUNCIL IS NARROW-MINDED, *CHOOSING* NOT TO SEE.

THE CYCLOPS SAW PRETTY WELL, THAT'S NOT EVEN A *METAPHOR,* DAMN IT--

VICKI VALE.

IS SOMEONE--?!

IS SOMEONE *IN* HERE?!

VICKI VALE.

I'M CALLING 911--!

IT WON'T WORK.

BESIDES, THERE'S NOBODY HERE AND NOTHING TO WORRY ABOUT--

--TO MAKE A CLASSICAL ALLUSION OF MY OWN.

I'VE BEEN VISITING SOME OF BRUCE'S OLD *GIRLFRIENDS*--

--FUNNY YOU SHOULD MENTION *EYES.*

GIRLFRIEND BODY PARTS

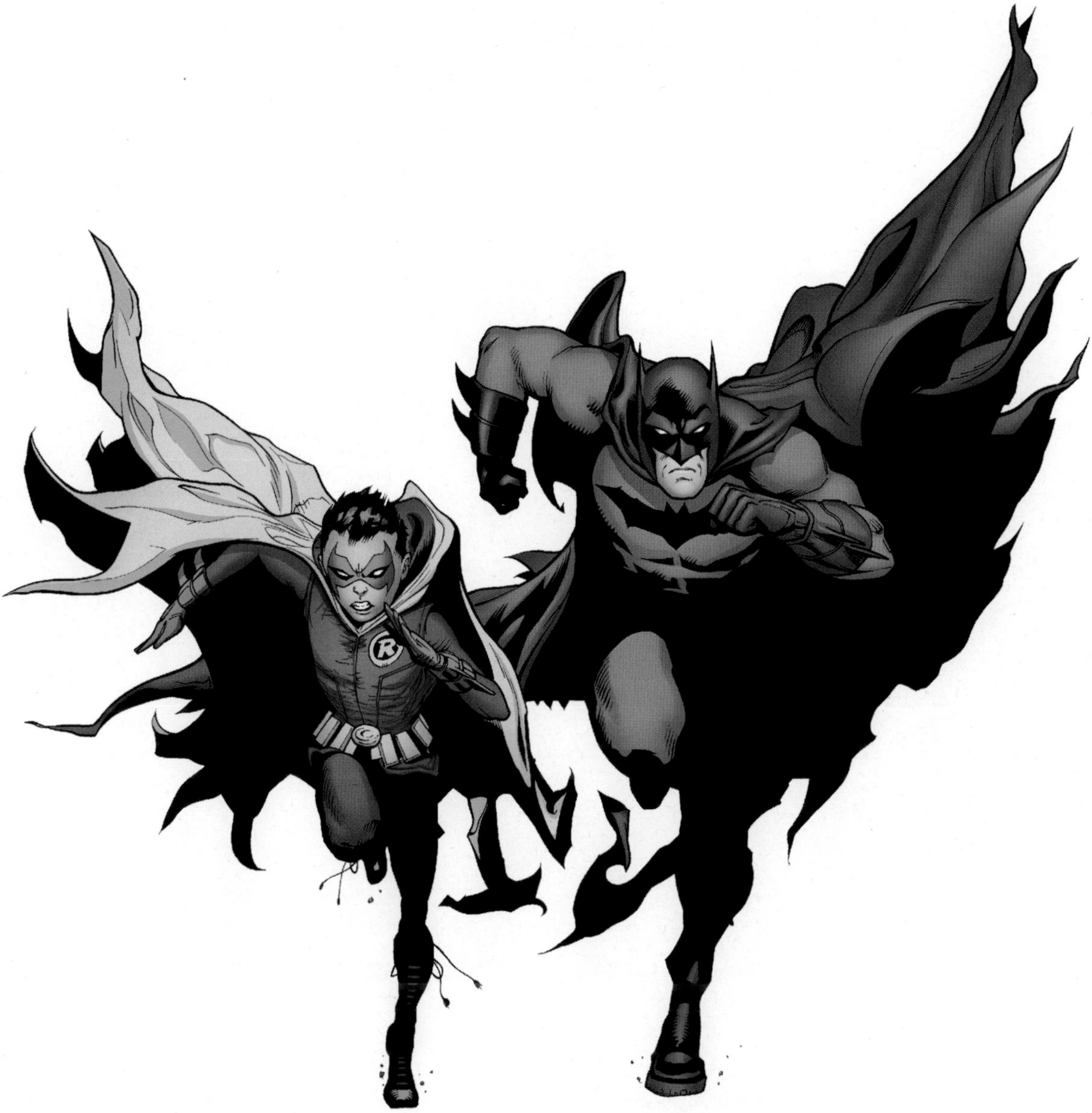

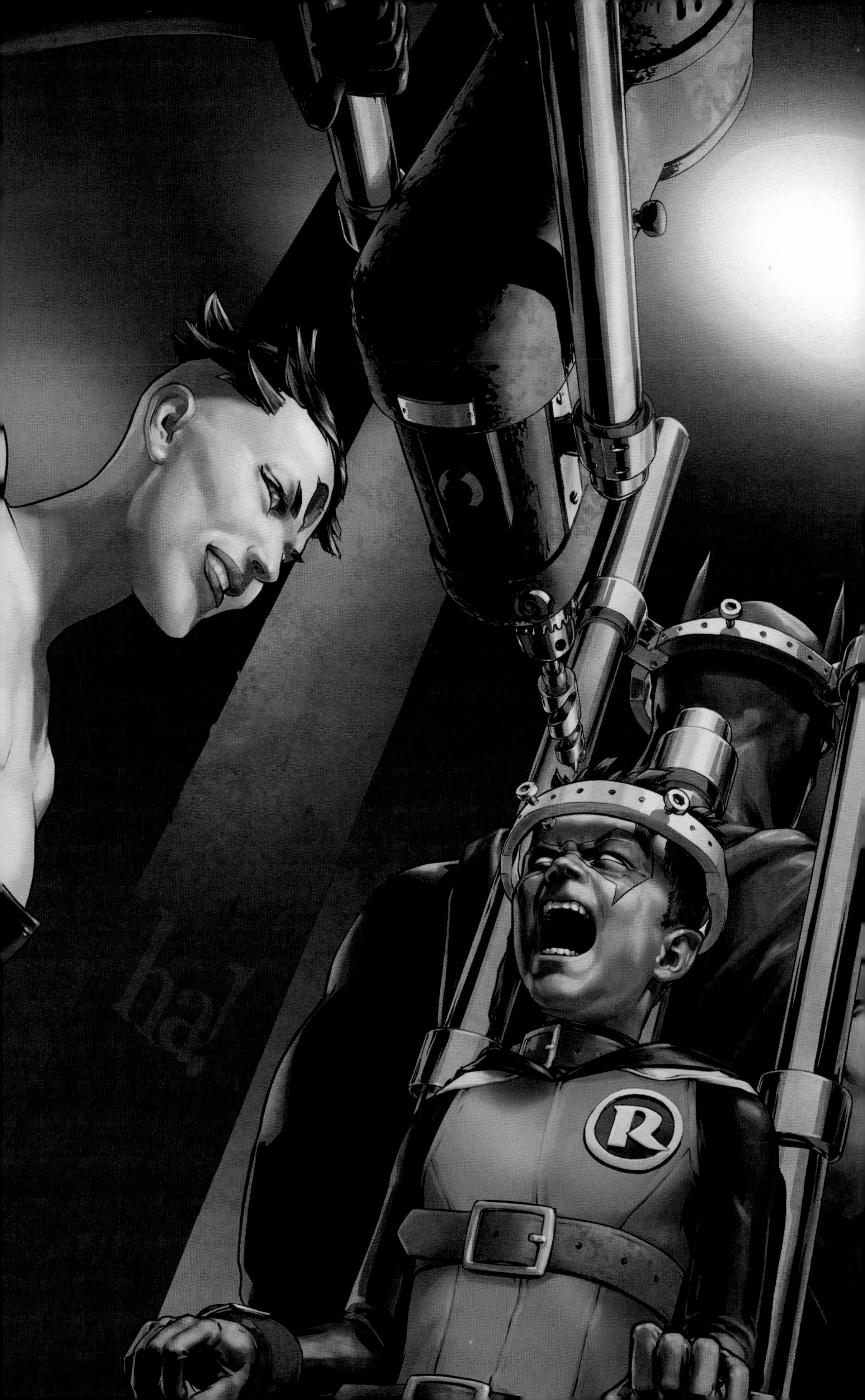
ha!

WHERE IS VICKI VALE?! WHAT HAVE YOU *DONE* TO HER?!

BATMAN AND ROBIN IN

THE SUM OF HER PARTS PART 3

PAUL CORNELL *writer* SCOTT McDANIEL *penciller*
ROB HUNTER *inker* ALEX SINCLAIR *colorist* PATRICK BROSSEAU *letterer*
Covers by PATRICK GLEASON *with* MARK IRWIN *and* GENE HA

NOTHING.

GIRLFRIEND BODY PARTS

BECAUSE THESE ARE CARDBOARD--

--AND THIS IS DOGFOOD.

BRUCE SAID I'D HURT HER, DIDN'T HE?! HE'S STILL MISSING THE POINT!

HE THINKS THIS IS ABOUT JEALOUSY!

LIKE I'D ATTACK INNOCENT WOMEN! WAY AHEAD OF HIM!

BUT STILL DISAPPOINTED!

IF SHE WAS A *PROPER* PSYCHOTIC, THIS WOULD BE *MUCH* LESS TIRESOME.

SO WHERE *IS* MISS VALE?

NOT IN ANY DANGER.

I'M NOT *AGAINST* KILLING--AS YOU'LL FIND OUT--

--BUT NOT WHEN IT'S *STUPID.*

MR. WAYNE SENT A MESSAGE--

OH, HE'S SO *SORRY,* RIGHT?

HE'D WANT TO MAKE THIS RIGHT. WHATEVER HE CAN DO.

WHATEVER YOU *NEED.*

"HE'D WANT!" NOT THAT HE'S *TOLD* YOU!

I *NEED* DIGNITY, RECOGNITION, *PERSONHOOD.*

I NEED BRUCE TO STOP SENDING *ASSISTANTS,* TO STOP NOT *BEING* HERE.

HE WOULD HAVE COME HIMSELF--

BUT THERE'S SOMETHING *MORE IMPORTANT.* FOR A PLAYBOY BILLIONAIRE.

LISTEN--!

--IT ISN'T *LIKE* THAT!

WE CAN OFFER YOU MEDICAL HELP, PSYCHIATRIC HELP...

IN *THIS* CITY?

THERE'S *NOTHING* YOU CAN DO TO HELP.

NO *ACTION* YOU CAN TAKE TO EVEN THE SCALES.

NO *STANCE* THAT WILL MAKE YOU *COOL* OR *REASONABLE*.

THEN WHY ARE WE TALKING?

IT'S NOT ABOUT THE CONVERSATION.

OBVIOUSLY. YOU'RE PLAYING FOR TIME.

WOW--

--YOU'RE *REALLY* NOT--

--CONCERNED ABOUT WALKING INTO TRAPS--

--ARE YOU?

THREE MINUTES OF EXPOSURE--

AND YOU'RE OUT. I HAD TO GET YOU AWAY FROM THE WINDOW.

YOU DON'T LACK EGO--

--ENTERING MY WORLD, TIME AFTER TIME.

UNPROTECTED.

YOU--!

NOTHING TO BE DONE.

NOTHING AT ALL.

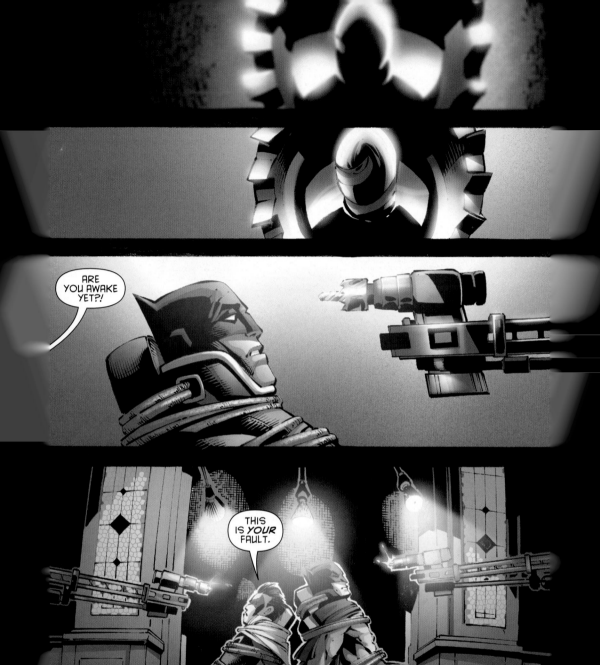

ARE YOU AWAKE YET?!

THIS IS *YOUR* FAULT.

NO QUESTIONS?

NO, THAT WOULD BE A SIGN OF WEAKNESS.

I'LL EXPLAIN.

IF YOU'RE GOING TO TELL BRUCE HOW I FEEL--

--YOU NEED TO *KNOW* HOW I FEEL.

IN FACT, YOU NEED THIS *EXACTLY* AS MUCH AS YOU NEED A HOLE IN THE HEAD!

TREPANATION, IT'S CALLED.

THE RUSH OF OXYGEN TO THE BRAIN. THE SUDDEN CLARITY. I READ THAT IT STOPS MALE RAGE. NO MORE *HORMONES!* YOU'LL THINK LIKE A *GIRL!*

UNFORTUNATELY, I'M NOT USED TO POWER TOOLS.

BUT THESE DAYS I'VE GOT QUITE A FEW *BATMEN* TO GET THROUGH.

SO I CAN KEEP TRYING UNTIL I GET IT RIGHT!

WHIRRRRRRR!

WHIRRRRRRR!

WHIRRRRRRR!

IT'LL TAKE ABOUT *THREE MINUTES* FOR THE DRILLS TO REACH YOUR FOREHEADS.

DO YOU THINK BRUCE WILL MIND MY SENDING HIS BATMEN BACK TO HIM WITH *HOLES* IN THEM?

NO REPLY. HERE'S ANOTHER DETAIL.

WHIRRRRRRR!

THE FLOOR SLIDES BACK AND FORTH.

YOU CAN PUSH ON THE CHAIRS.

WHIRRRRRRR!

IF YOU CAN'T TRUST ME TO DO IT RIGHT--

--TO JUST *GENTLY* PENETRATE YOUR THICK SKULLS--

--THEN ONE OF YOU CAN PUSH BACK--

--AND SEND THE DRILL *DEEP* INTO THE OTHER'S BRAIN.

OR...

...ONE OF US COULD PUSH *FORWARD.*

AND *MOCK* YOU WITH HIS DEATH.

WOW--!

--NO FEAR FROM THIS LITTLE SOLDIER!

DEATH BEFORE SISSIFICATION!

I HAVE *NO IDEA* WHAT YOU'RE TALKING ABOUT.

NO? I THINK *THIS* IS A GOOD TEST OF WHAT'S *MISSING.*

DID BRUCE INSTILL *LOYALTY* TO EACH OTHER IN YOU?

OR DO YOU FEEL YOU'RE ALL AS DISPOSABLE AS I WAS?

WILL THERE BE PLEADING IN SEARCH OF THE FEELINGS YOU'RE WORRIED I LACK?

APPEALS TO A MATERNAL SENSE? TO OUR *ALL* HAVING BEEN SCREWED BY BRUCE WAYNE?

NOT LITERALLY IN EITHER CASE. OBVIOUSLY.

WHIRRRRRRR.

RRRRRRR!

OR WILL THERE BE *INSULTS* ABOUT GAPS LIKE THAT?

WILL YOU CALL ME HEARTLESS? MINDLESS?

LACKING APPROPRIATE *WEAKNESS?*

I KNOW WHAT THIS IS *REALLY* ABOUT, UNA...

WHIRRRRRRR!

...WE'LL *NEVER* TELL YOU OUR SECRET IDENTITIES!

YOU'RE NOT ANYONE I CARE ABOUT.

I'M NOT GOING TO STOP THIS TO TAKE OFF YOUR MASK.

WHIRRRRRRR!

DO YOU THINK WE REALLY LEAP INTO TRAPS WITHOUT BACK-UP?

OTHERS ARE ON THEIR WAY...

THAT'S THE SAME PLOY JAMES BOND USED IN *GOLDFINGER*, ISN'T IT?!

NO, MR. BATMAN, I EXPECT YOU TO BE ENLIGHTENED!

AND/OR DIE.

WHIRRRRRRR!

YOU KNOW WE'RE JUST PAWNS TO BRUCE WAYNE!

HE'LL SACRIFICE US ALL WITHOUT LOSING ANY SLEEP!

IF YOU REALLY BELIEVED THAT, YOU WOULDN'T SAY IT OUT LOUD.

DAMN IT...

...ALL RIGHT.

I'LL SAY WHAT YOU WANT TO HEAR!

YOU *DON'T KNOW* WHAT I WANT TO HEAR.

BUT GO ON. TRY TO FILL ANOTHER VOID.

YOU'RE *RIGHT.*

THAT'S THE AWFUL THING.

WE ALL *KNOW* YOU'RE RIGHT.

BRUCE WAYNE *CERTAINLY* DOES.

WHIRRRRRRR!

BUT WE WANT THERE TO BE SOMETHING WE CAN *DO!*

NOT SOMETHING WE HAVE TO *NOT* DO!

BUT WHAT IF THERE'S *NOTHING?*

I WON'T PUSH BACK.

NOT EVEN AS A *REFLEX*.

ARE YOU REALLY PRETENDING THIS WON'T KILL US?!

WHIRRRRRRR!

WHIRRRRRR!

ISN'T *THAT* "STUPID"?! TO PASS THIS OFF AS *HALF* A DEATH TRAP?!

STILL TRYING. TRYING TO PUT HALVES IN MY HEAD INSTEAD OF ZEROES ISN'T THE KEY. THERE *ISN'T* A KEY.

IS THAT ALL YOU ARE, *HURTING* BECAUSE YOU WERE *HURT*?!

WHIRRRRRRR!

IS THAT ALL YOU--?!

--AHHHHHHHH!!!!

SHREGKK!

WHAT?

SHREGKK!

NO.

THAT'S *NOT* ALL I AM.

THE DRILL BITS WERE PAPIER-MACHE.

YOU'VE ACTUALLY SURPRISED ME--

--I THOUGHT YOU WERE *LYING*.

THAT THE WHOLE OF BATMAN, INC. WOULD BE HERE BY NOW.

NO...

...I ENJOY THE LUXURY THESE DAYS...

...OF WORKING *WITHOUT* A SAFETY NET.

IT'S NOT IMPORTANT. I HOPE.

AREN'T YOU SCHOLARS OF DETECTIVE FICTION?

NEVER HEARD OF "THE RED-HEADED LEAGUE"?

WAIT. A STORY WHERE THE WHOLE POINT IS--

NOT WHAT IT SEEMS TO BE.

A DISTRACTION. THE RIVER ROBBERY CREW--

YOU'RE NOT AS QUICK AS I AM--

--BUT YOU ARE QUICK.

IN THE LAST FEW HOURS--

"--MY PEOPLE--

"--FOLLOWING MY GAME PLAN--

"--WILL HAVE *DEALT* WITH EVERY SINGLE ONE."

SO THIS WAS ALL A FEINT? THE WHOLE POSE--

WAS TO GET AS MANY BATMEN AS POSSIBLE RUNNING AFTER *ME.* SOLVING THE CRIME. COMING TO SAVE YOU.

WHILE I GOT THE *PRACTICAL* BUSINESS DONE.

YOU LOOKED FOR A TYPICAL SUPER VILLAIN--

--YOU FOUND THE *ABSENCE* OF ONE.

AH-AH!

ROBIN, NO!

YOU THINK I MIGHT SURRENDER NOW?

NO NO *NO.*

DON'T IMAGINE I DIDN'T *MEAN* ALL I SAID--

--THAT I DIDN'T *ENJOY* PENETRATING YOUR CONSCIOUSNESS.

I AM BRUCE WAYNE'S BLIND SPOT.

I AM WHAT HE WON'T SEE.

I *NEED* HIM TO *MISS* ME.

BUT I WON'T MISS--

--MYSELF.

NO!

BLAM!

I-I CAN'T SEE--

THERE'S NO SIGN...

NOBODY--

NO CORPSE.

NOTHING.

THE BATBUNKER

WHEN WE WERE IN THAT DEATH TRAP, YOU DIDN'T PUSH BACKWARDS.

NO. SO WHAT DO YOU SAY?

"GOOD."

THE G.C.P.D. FOUND THE CHEMIST. LOCKED IN A DOUGHNUT FACTORY.

AH, THE HOLES IN THE MIDDLE. SHE IS NOT WITHOUT A SENSE OF HUMOR.

NOR IS SHE WITHOUT MERCY.

THAT'S WHAT MAKES THIS SO... DIFFICULT.

SHE'S NOT WHAT WE NORMALLY DEAL WITH.

SHE...KIND OF HAS A POINT.

BRUCE ALWAYS TOOK CARE--

--BUT HE NEVER HAD THE MOST HUMANE PRIORITIES.

LOOK AT WHO HE MADE--

"--A BATMAN WHO'S *ENJOYING* THE THRILL OF BEING EXPENDABLE.

"AND A ROBIN WHO'S WILLING TO *DIE* FOR THE CAUSE.

"UNA NEMO LOOKED INTO THE *HEART* OF WHAT BRUCE DID--

"--WITHOUT EVEN MEANING TO. NOT *THIS* TIME.

"MAYBE SHE FOUND SOMETHING *MISSING.*"

END?

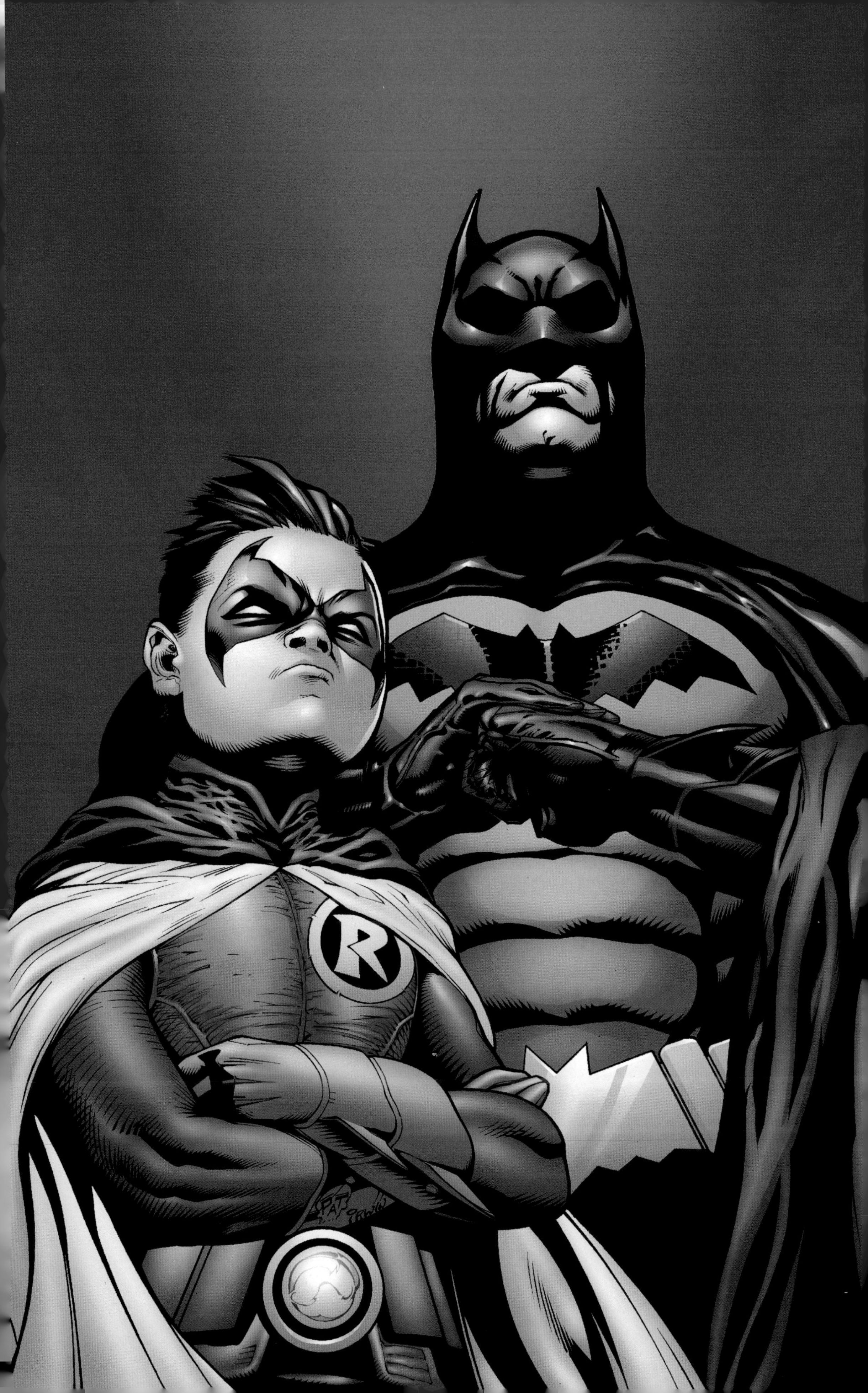

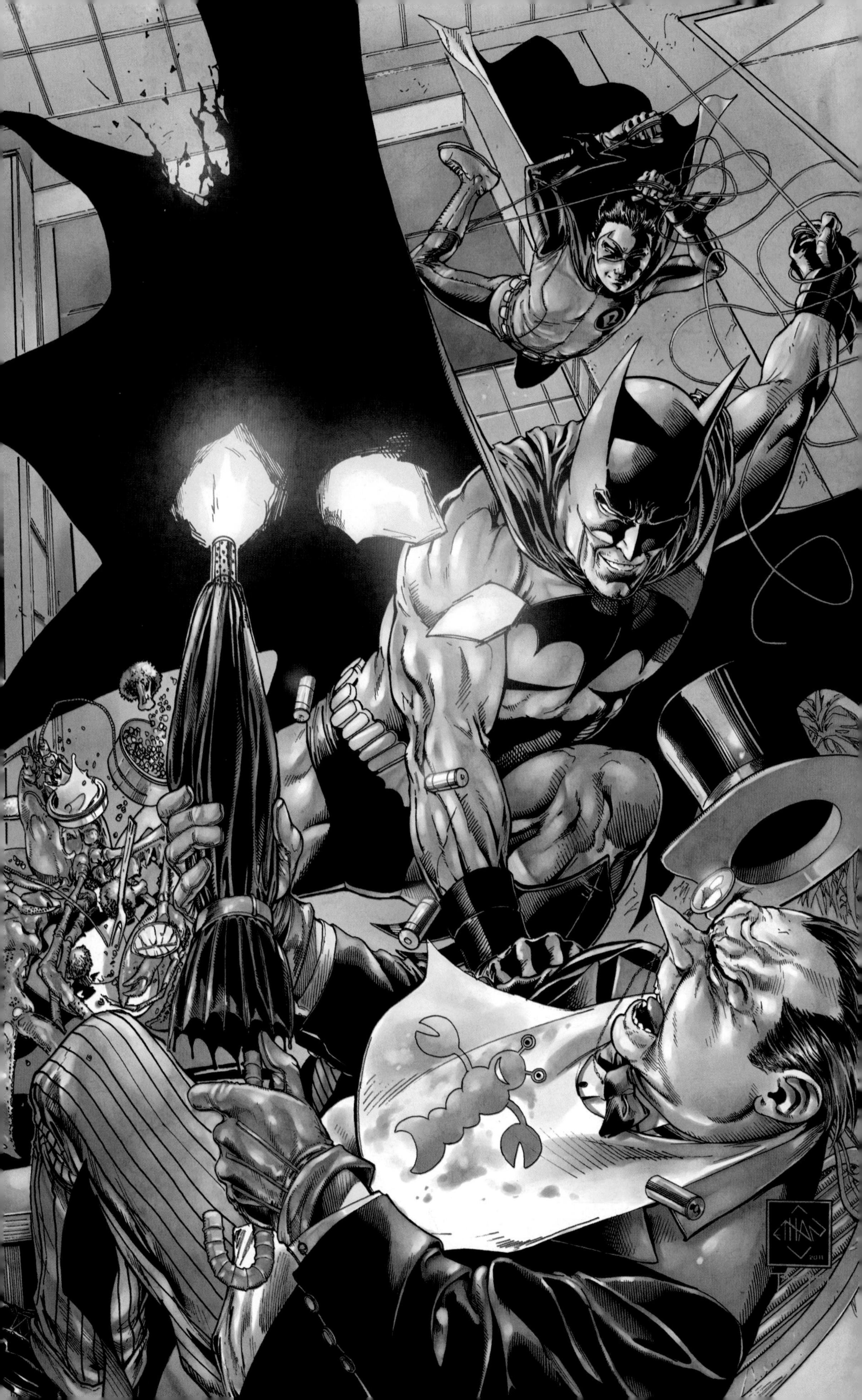

GOTHAM CITY. WAYNE MANOR.

IT'S BEEN QUITE SOME TIME SINCE ALL YOU BOYS WERE UNDER ONE ROOF WITHOUT YOUR UNIFORMS.

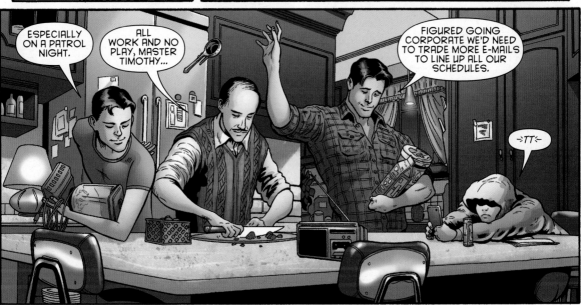

ESPECIALLY ON A PATROL NIGHT.

ALL WORK AND NO PLAY, MASTER TIMOTHY...

FIGURED GOING CORPORATE WE'D NEED TO TRADE MORE E-MAILS TO LINE UP ALL OUR SCHEDULES.

÷TT÷

DID YOU TOSS IN SOME OVALTINE, ALFIE?

AS ALWAYS.

HEARD THE HEAD HONCHO WAS DOING A LITTLE TANGO OF DEATH WITH A HOT LATIN NUMBER A FEW WEEKS BACK.

YEAH, HE'S STARTING A NEW TV SHOW TOO--DANCING WITH THE BATS.

YOU GUYS GOT A NEW SCREEN! IS THAT ONLY A 50 INCH?

I DO BELIEVE IT'S THE SIZE OF A CAR AND WILL SUIT OUR NEEDS.

I THINK IT'S A 70.

HEY, TIM, I HOPE YOU ADJUSTED IT AND DIDN'T LEAVE IT ON THE FACTORY SPECS.

SURE, IT WAS ON THE TOP OF MY "LIST OF THINGS TO DO," DICK.

MIND IF I SCROLL THROUGH THE MENU AND ADJUST THE COLOR LEVELS?

HERE, KNOCK YOURSELF OUT.

FAP

GLAD YOU COULD ALL MAKE IT.

FLIK

OPEN YOUR MIND, DAMIAN. THE MOVIE'S GOT A LOT OF SWORDPLAY AND NO CGI. YOU'LL LOVE IT.

YOU'RE GONNA TORTURE US WITH SOME ANCIENT BLACK-AND-WHITE MOVIE, AREN'T YOU?

UM...BRUCE, YOU SURE YOU WANT TO WATCH THIS?

IT MAY HAVE BEEN THE *WORST NIGHT* OF MY LIFE, DICK, BUT UP UNTIL *CHILL* STEPPED OUT OF THE SHADOWS, IT WAS ONE OF THE *BEST DAYS* OF MY LIFE.

WASN'T OFTEN I GOT TO SPEND *EVERY* WAKING MINUTE WITH *BOTH* MY MOTHER AND FATHER. THE WHOLE DAY FELT SPECIAL.

LOOKING BACK, THIS MOVIE NOT ONLY MARKED AN ENDING, BUT A BEGINNING...

...OF A NEW ROAD...A NEW PATH...

SO IT KIND OF FEELS LIKE THE RIGHT TIME TO SEE IT AGAIN...

THE MARK OF
Zorro

PLAY

CHAPTERS

ORIGINAL THEATRICAL TRAILER

BONUS FEATURES

...WITH THE WHOLE FAMILY.

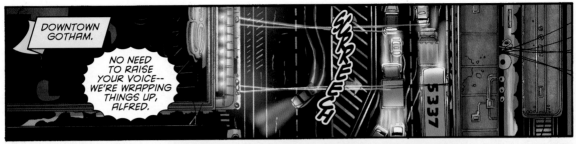

DOWNTOWN GOTHAM.

NO NEED TO RAISE YOUR VOICE-- WE'RE WRAPPING THINGS UP, ALFRED.

I SHOULD HOPE SO. YOU ARE RUNNING EXTREMELY LATE THIS EVENING.

AND CAN YOU BOTH PLEASE STAY PUT FOR FIVE SECONDS SO THIS GPS CAN GET A LOCK ON YOUR LOCATION?

OKAY, FIVE SECONDS, YOU GOT IT.

->UUGGH<-

I SURE HOPE THOSE WERE BABY TEETH.

THE WIRE TOO TIGHT?

->NNN<--- YEAH--CAN'T FEEL MY ARMS--

GOOD.

SORRY TO PUNCH AND RUN...

...BUT OUR RIDE'S HERE.

VRRRROOM

WHY DO *I* HAVE TO CALL IT A NIGHT WHEN YOU DO?

THEY'RE CALLED RULES. LEARN 'EM, LIVE 'EM. WE ALL DID.

WELL, I'M NOT PUTTING ON A MONKEY SUIT AND GOING TO THIS THING.

AN EVENING WITHOUT A TEN-YEAR-OLD PAIN-IN-THE-ASS BY MY SIDE-- WHAT WILL I DO?

ALFRED, I CAN NEVER GET THESE DAMN BOW TIES...

LEAN FORWARD, SIR.

WHAT AM I LATE FOR?

A NEW PRODUCTION OF *DAS RHEINGOLD* SPONSORED BY THE MARTHA WAYNE ARTS FOUNDATION.

WILL I LIKE IT?

DID YOU ENJOY BUGS BUNNY IN "WHAT'S OPERA, DOC?" AS A BOY?

YEP.

THEN I ASSUME YOU WILL ENJOY THIS TREMENDOUSLY.

ALFRED, DID YOU BRING--

YOUR SHOES, SIR.

MARTHA WAYNE FOUNDATION PRESENTATION

DAS RHEINGOLD

GOOD EVENING, RICHARD.

HI, LUCIUS. HOW'S YOUR DAUGHTER, TAM, DOING?

SHE'S DOING FINE NOW, THANKS FOR ASKING.

MR. GRAYSON, I'M BETTY TICORAS, THE FOUNDATION'S PUBLICIST--COULD I HAVE YOU STEP OVER TO THE PAPARAZZI FOR A FEW CANDID SHOTS?

UM, SURE, BETTY, NO PROBLEM.

WHAT IS IT, RICHARD? IS EVERYTHING ALL RIGHT?

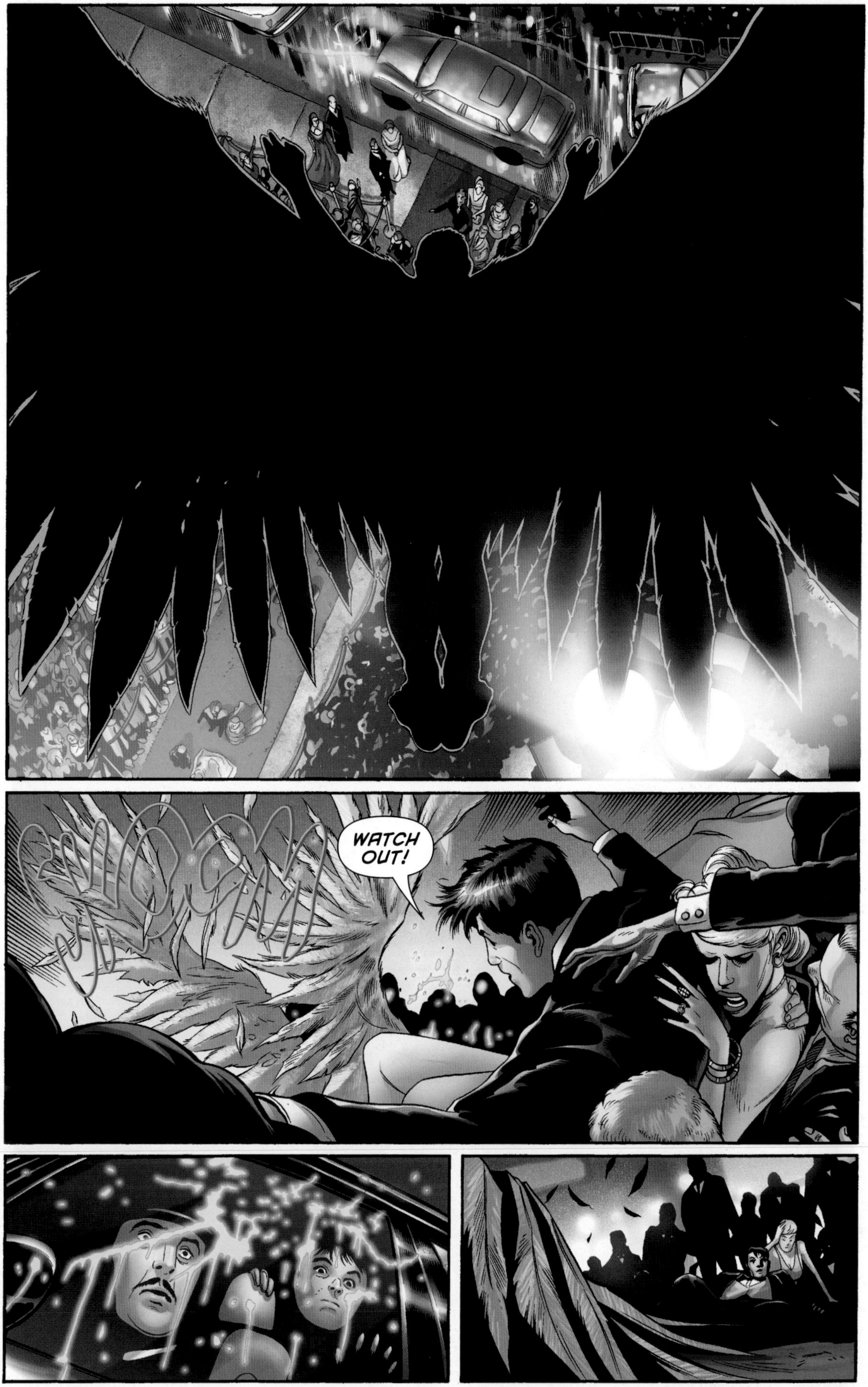
WATCH OUT!

GOOD GOD...

I DON'T THINK SO, LUCIUS.

Tree of Blood

DARK KNIGHT vs. WHITE KNIGHT PART 1 OF 3

PETER J. TOMASI: WRITER
PATRICK GLEASON: PENCILLER
MICK GRAY: INKER ALEX SINCLAIR: COLORIST
PATRICK BROSSEAU: LETTERER
GLEASON AND IRWIN: COVER
ETHAN VAN SCIVER: VARIANT COVER

GUESS YOU MOVE TO THE FRONT OF THE AUTOPSY LINE WHEN A MAYOR AND SOME MOVIE STARS ALMOST GET KILLED BY A FALLING ANGEL, COMMISSIONER.

DEFINITELY A PLUS WHEN IT COMES TO HELPING ME PRIORITIZE MY CASELOAD, BATMAN.

I.D.ING POTATO HEAD HERE IS GOING TO TAKE SOME TIME.

SHOW SOME RESPECT FOR THE DEAD, ROBIN.

MY BAD. I MEANT *MISTER* POTATO HEAD.

NEVER TALK AS FLIPPANT LIKE THAT IN FRONT OF ME AND A INNOCENT VICTIM AGAIN, OR THIS'LL BE THE LAST TIME I LET YOU TAG ALONG.

WE CLEAR, *KID?*

SURE, *OLD MAN,* WE'RE CLEAR.

AND I DON'T *TAG* ALONG.

HOW MANY STORIES DID HE FALL?

EIGHTY.

THE EXO-SKELETON OF THE WINGS IS HOLLOW-- THEY'RE TUBES.

GLOWING BLOOD WAS INSIDE THEM.

HIS ENTIRE POSTERIOR IS *PULVERIZED*--

ALONG WITH THE BACK OF HIS SKULL-- *DISTORTING* HIS FACIAL FEATURES.

I'M SURE I'LL FIND TRACES OF THE ADHESIVE THAT HELD THE WINGS IN PLACE WHEN I GET THE TOX AND CULTURE REPORTS BACK.

I SEE HE WENT THE EXTRA MILE TO KEEP HIS IDENTITY CONCEALED.

YEAH, CORONER TOLD ME HE USED SOME KIND OF ACID. BURNED HIS OWN DAMN FINGERPRINTS OFF.

AND HIS FEET, TOO.

WHY WOULD HE DO THAT?

BABIES' FOOTPRINTS ARE TAKEN AT BIRTH.

HE LITERALLY COVERED ALL HIS *TRACKS* BEFORE COMMITTING SUICIDE.

ROBIN, SCAN THE OTHER SIDE OF THE VICTIM'S FACE WHILE I SCAN THE FRONT.

COMMISSIONER, WE'RE GOING TO TRY TO DIGITALLY RECONSTRUCT HIS HEAD AND THEN CROSSCHECK HIS FACE AGAINST THE CITY'S SECURITY CAMERA DATABASES BECAUSE--

--IF OUR "ANGEL" HERE HAS EVER WALKED A GOTHAM STREET OR APPLIED FOR A PHOTO ID, WE SHOULD BE ABLE TO MATCH IT.

WELL, PUTTING A NAME TO THIS POOR SOUL'S FACE WILL BE THE FIRST--

->HHFF<-

THE MORE THINGS CHANGE, THE MORE THEY STAY THE SAME.

HELL OF A STATEMENT OR A HELL OF A WAY TO OFF YOURSELF.

OR BOTH.

WHAT ARE YOU *DOING?*

CHECKING FOR CAVITIES.

YOU'RE SUCH A SHOW-OFF.

YOU CAN TAKE THE BOY OUTTA THE CIRCUS, BUT NOT THE CIRCUS OUTTA THE BOY.

HERE. EVIDENCE TO GIVE TO GORDON, ALONG WITH *THIS.*

PLAIN AND SIMPLE, BATMAN. ANGEL WAS A JUMPER.

It's time to end the suffering. I will not add to the world's pain.

PLAIN AND SIMPLE, *HMM?*

SURE, ROBIN, THAT'LL BE THE--

SKREEEE!

AAARGH!

SAVE THEM!

--DAGGH!

SAVE THEM FROM THE LIGHT!

>UGGN!<

SKASH

THEIR SCREAMS--I CAN HEAR THEIR SCREAMS!

WHOSE SCREAMS?!

THEY'RE IN PAIN--CAN'T YOU HEAR THEM?!

YOU ARE KIRK LANGSTROM-- NOT MAN-BAT!

FIGHT IT, KIRK! TAKE CONTROL OF YOURSELF!

LISTEN TO THEM! MY CHILDREN ARE SCREAMING!

SKRASH

LAND, LANGSTROM-- NOW!

STOP MESSING AROUND WITH THIS GUY--

THIS FREAK'S GOING DOWN!

--AND CLIP HIS DAMN WINGS ALREADY!

THE LIGHT! STAY AWAY FROM THE LIGHT!

THEY'RE DYING-- SAVE THEM!

WHO'S DYING, LANGSTROM?!

YARRGH!

TALK TO ME, LANGSTROM-- WHAT LIGHT-- WHAT ARE YOU--

MAYBE US.

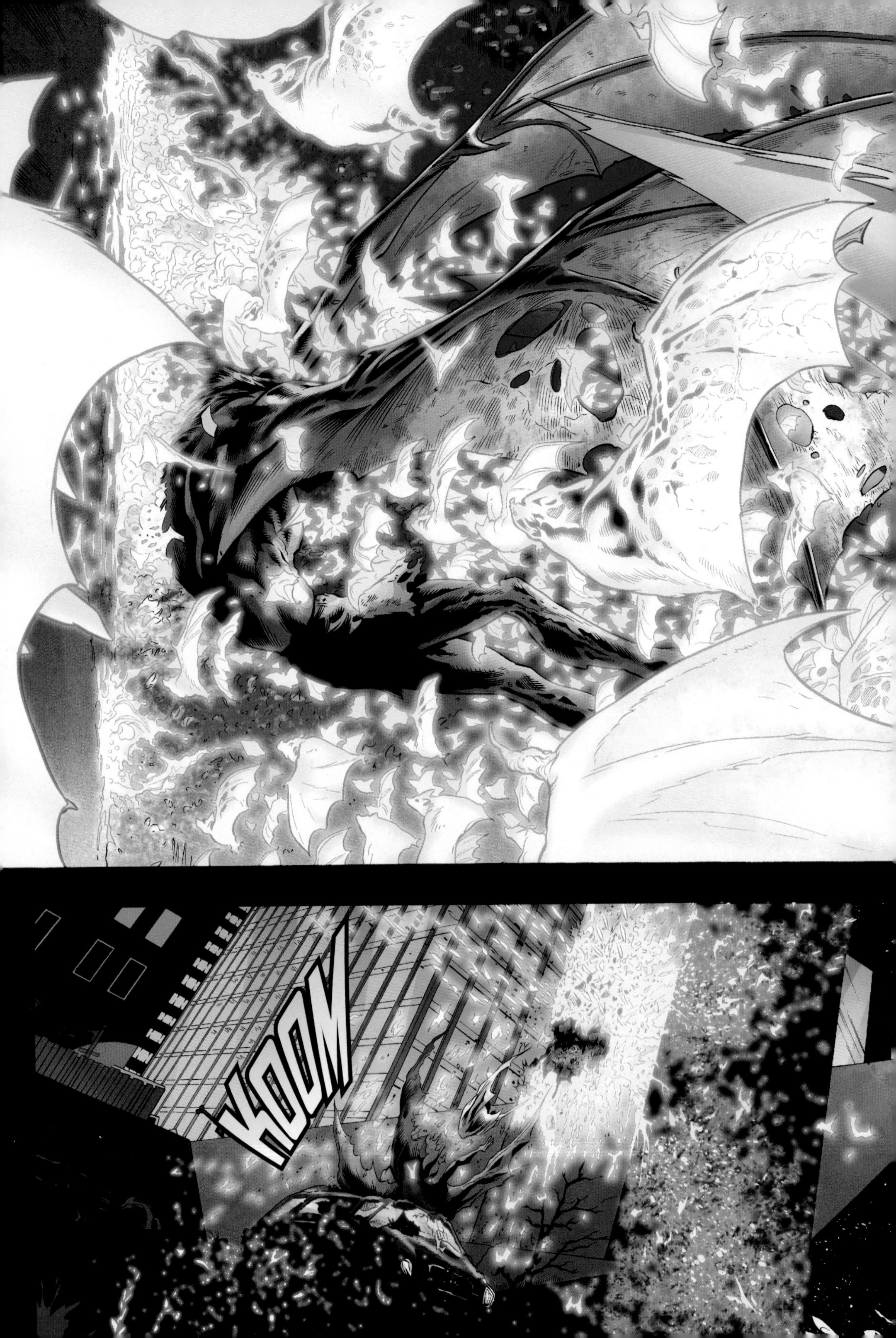
KOOM

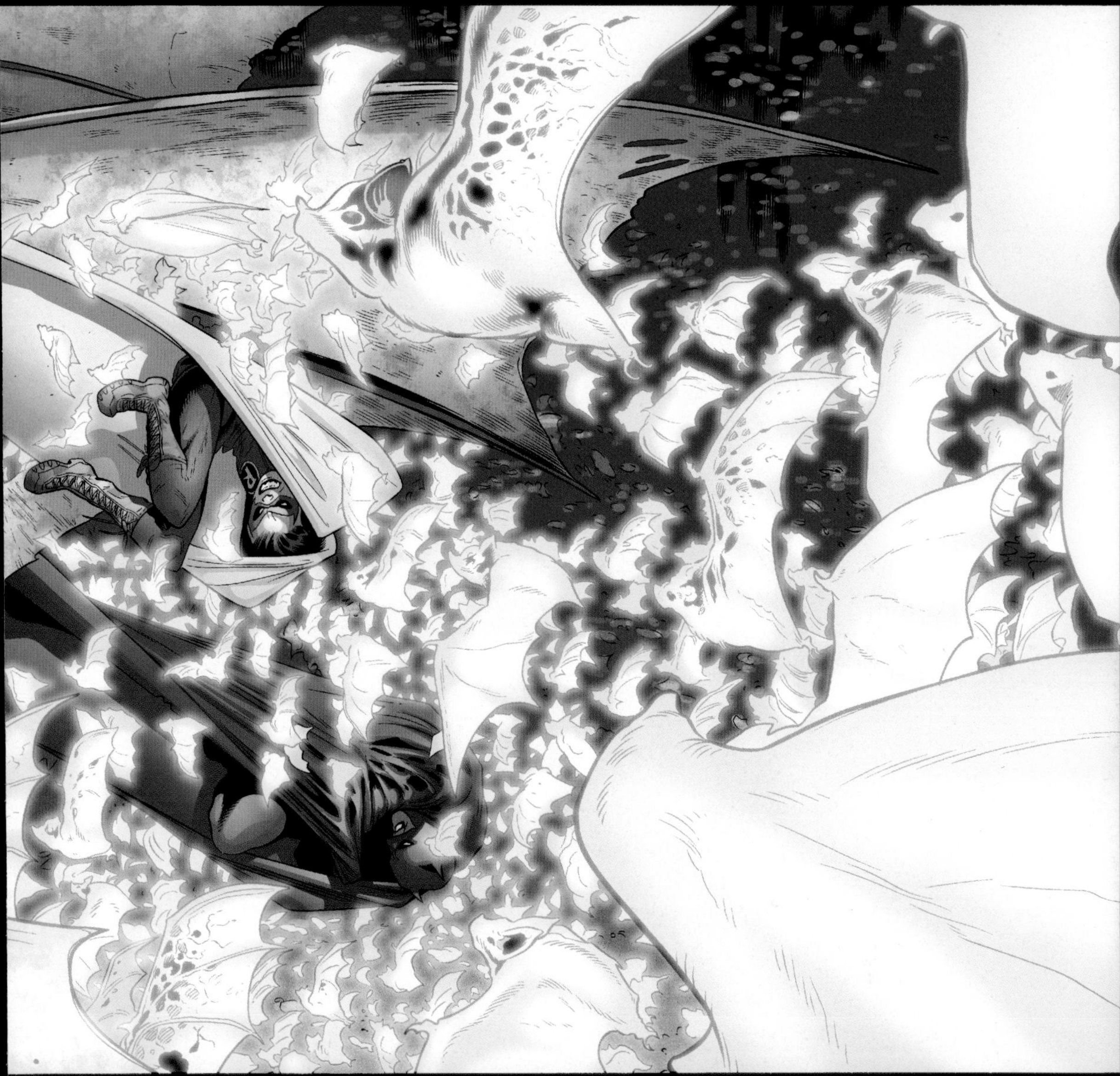
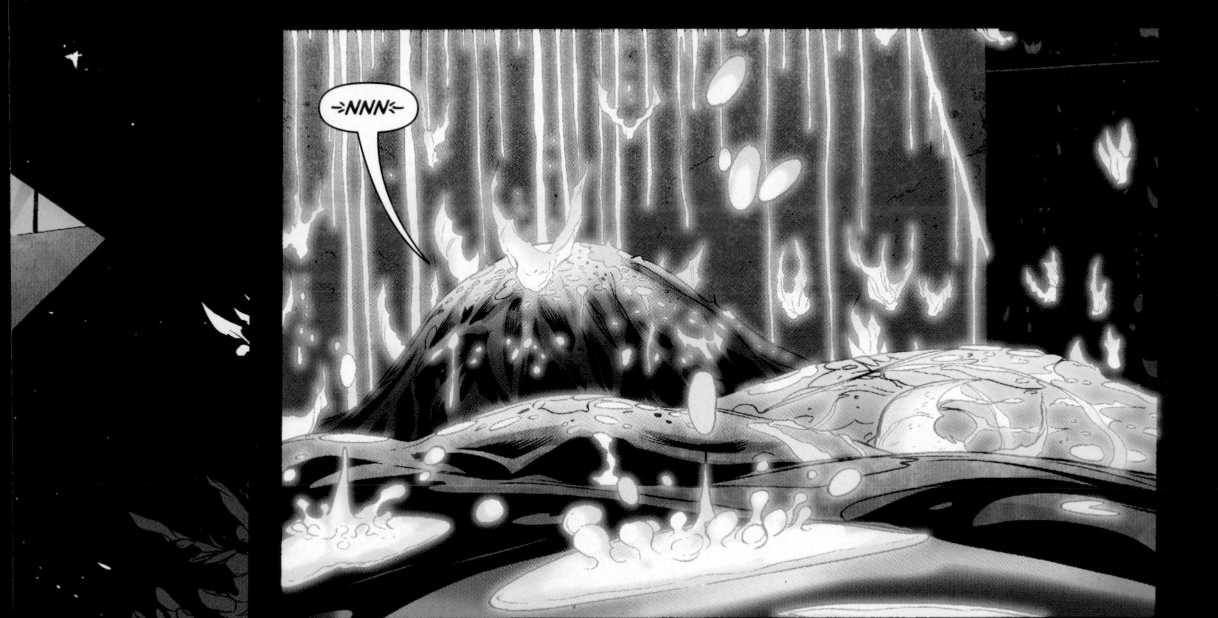
NNN

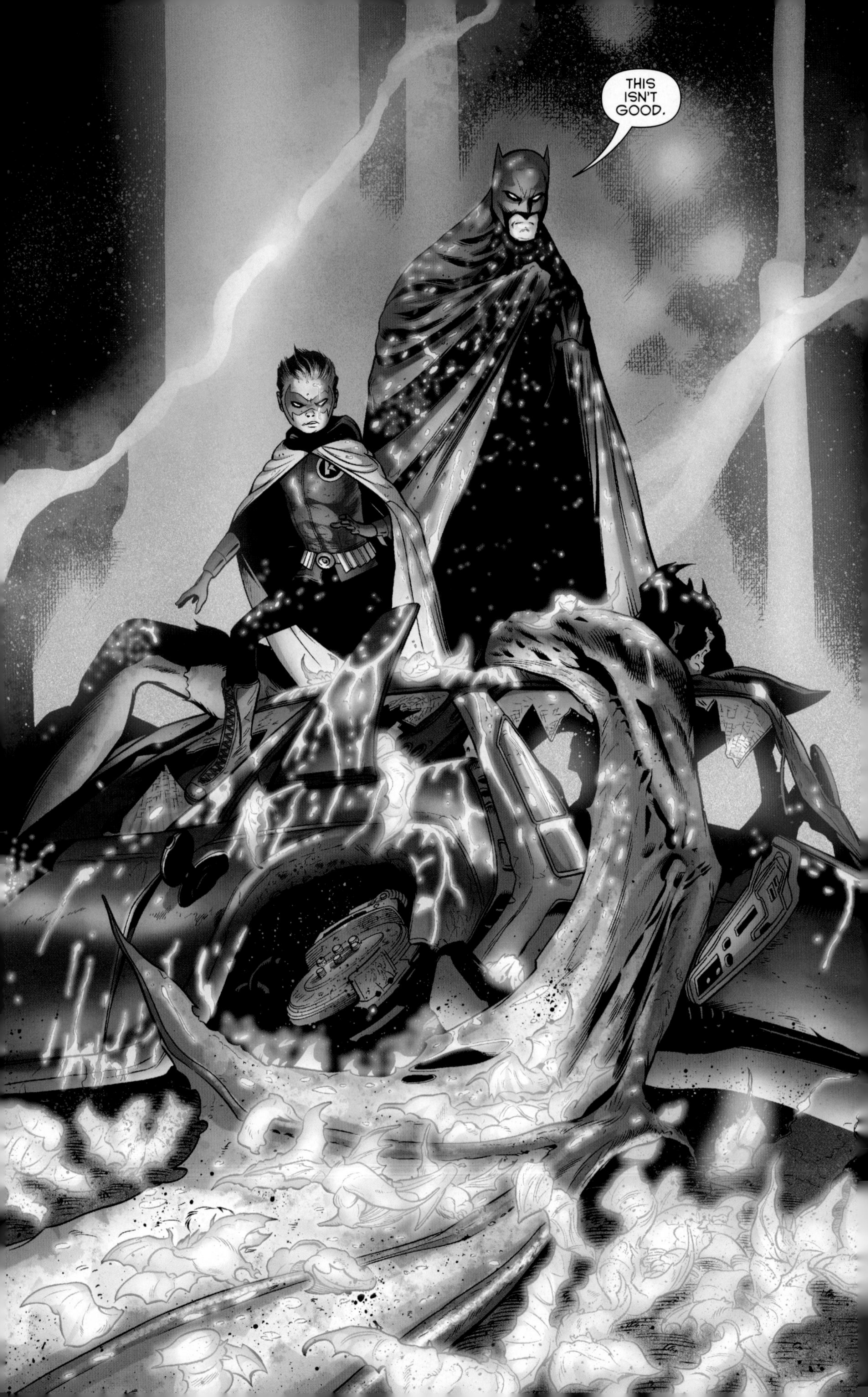
THIS ISN'T GOOD.

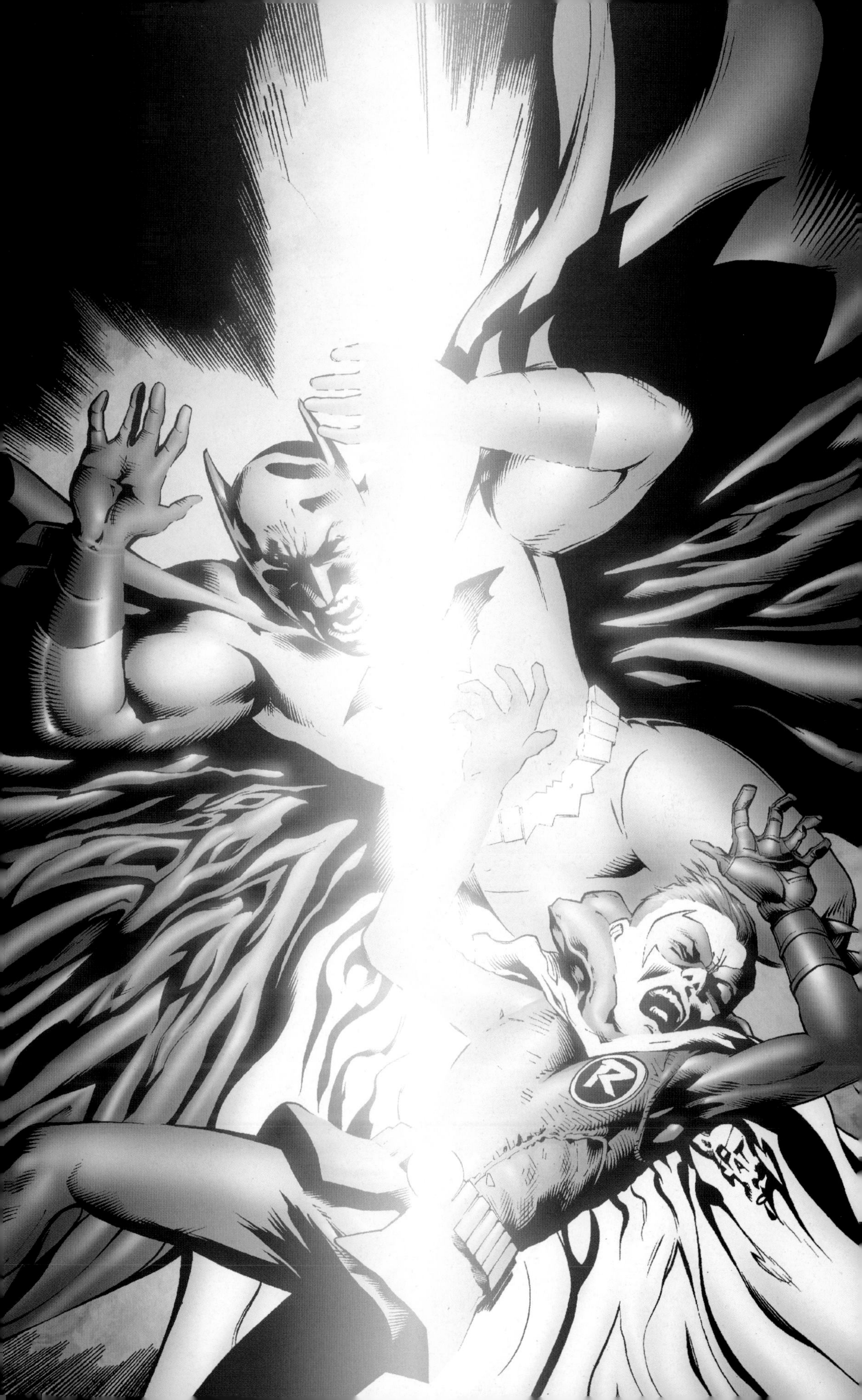

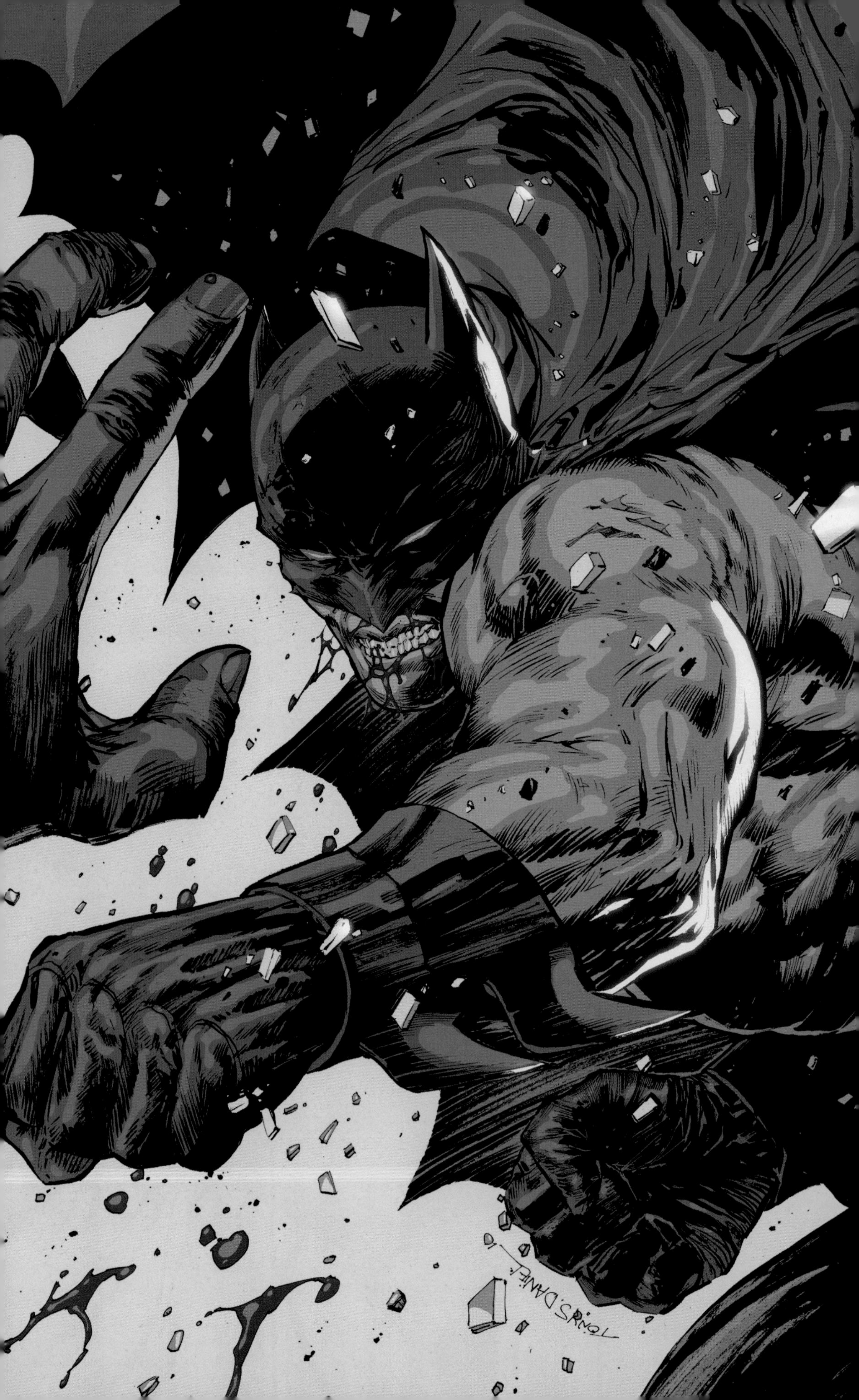
TONY S. DANIEL

I WANT YOU TO KNOW THAT I DO *ENVY* ALL OF YOU.

THE *LANGSTROM* FAMILY'S GOING TO SEE THINGS *I* NEVER WILL.

I'M DOING THIS *FOR* ALL OF YOU *AND* THIS BEAUTIFUL WORLD, *FRANCINE LANGSTROM.*

I'M OPENING A DOOR THAT WOULD HAVE BEEN FOREVER CLOSED--

--AND *SAVING YOU* AND YOUR CHILDREN FROM THE PIT.

DON'T WORRY, WE'VE GOT YOU!

Tree of Blood
DARK KNIGHT vs. WHITE KNIGHT PART 2 OF 3

PETER J. TOMASI: WRITER
PATRICK GLEASON: PENCILLER
MICK GRAY: INKER ALEX SINCLAIR: COLORIST
PATRICK BROSSEAU: LETTERER
GLEASON AND GRAY: COVER
TONY DANIEL: VARIANT COVER

LET'S GET THEM COVERED UP, ROBIN!

...AARON... REBECCA... ARE THEY--

YOUR KIDS ARE *SAFE*, FRANCINE, THEY'RE RIGHT HERE.

...B-BATMAN... THANK GOD...

FRANCINE, WHO DID THIS TO YOU?

YOUR HUSBAND, KIRK, ATTACKED US.

AS *MAN-BAT*?

I D-DON'T KNOW--A VOICE IN MY HEAD--HOW DID YOU FIND--

THE MICRO-TRACKER YOU IMPLANTED IN YOUR SHOULDER AFTER TALIA AL GHUL KIDNAPPED YOU FOR THE MAN-BAT SERUM--

--THE OUTSIDERS HAD THE FREQUENCY CODE FROM WHEN YOU WORKED WITH THEM.

SCREAMED SOMETHING ABOUT "SAVING HIS CHILDREN" WHILE HE TRIED TO BEAT US SENSELESS.

IF THERE'S ANYTHING YOU REMEMBER THAT CAN HELP US.

...I REMEMBER HOLDING SOMETHING... IT WAS HEAVY... BLINKING NUMBERS...

DID YOU LEAVE IT ON THE OTHER--

--BUILDING?

WHAT THE HELL--

FWOOOSH

YOUR WHITE KNIGHT IS HERE, GOTHAM!

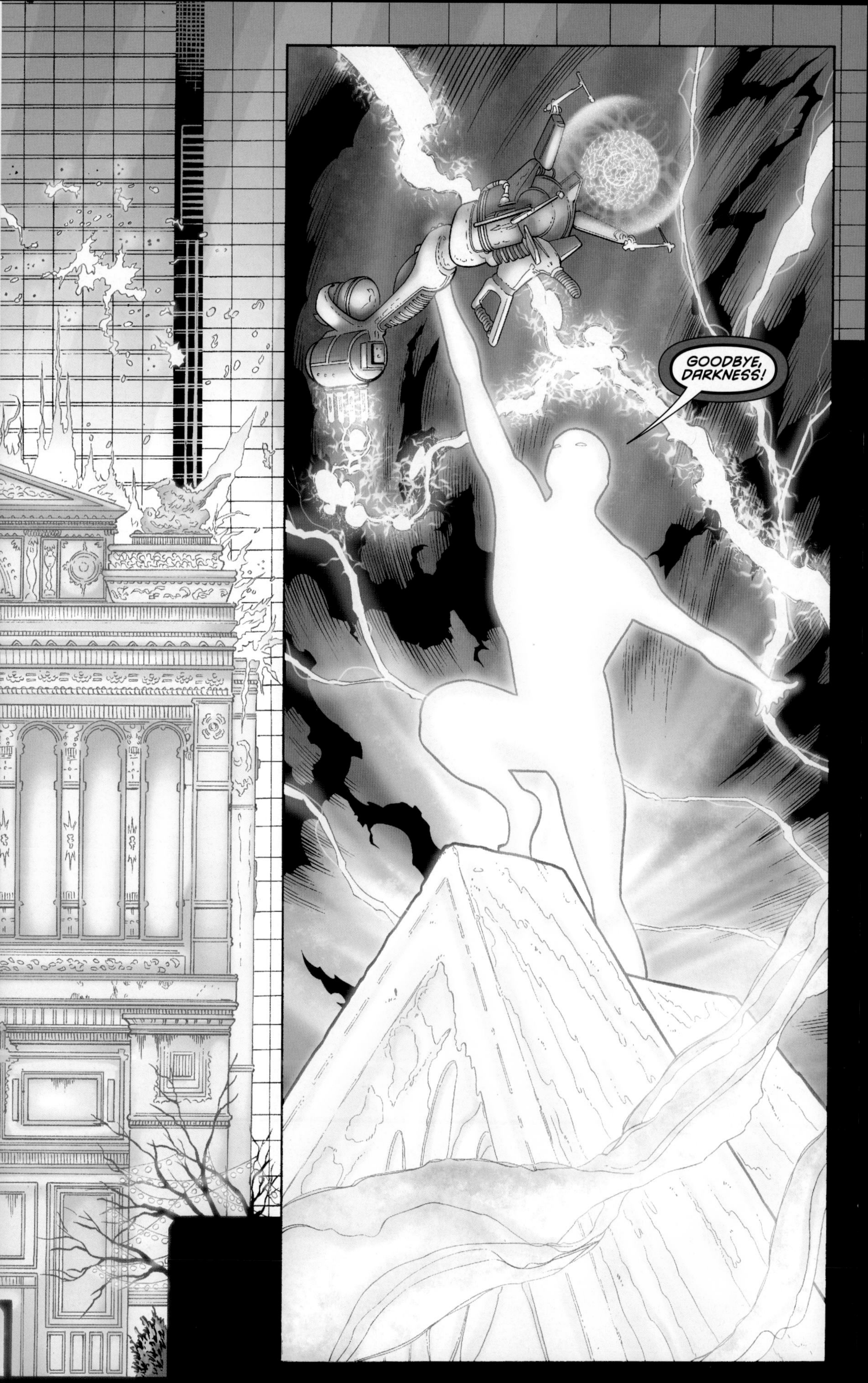
GOODBYE, DARKNESS!

POOM

POOM

EXCUSE US, FRANCINE, WHILE WE INTRODUCE OURSELVES TO THIS WALKING LIGHTBULB--

--BEFORE WE LOCK HIM UP!

STAY BACK!

GOTHAM NEEDS TO BE ILLUMINATED!

THIS IS THE FIRST STEP TO A BRIGHTER--

=UNFFF=

ACTUALLY IT'S YOUR LAST STEP BEFORE WE SHUT YOU UP AND SHIP YOU OFF!

NO ONE CAN STOP THE LIGHT!

IT WILL ALWAYS FIND A WAY TO BURN BACK THE EVIL IN OUR HEARTS!

ZMMMMM

ROBIN--HE'S BLOWING THE--

FRAWHOOSH

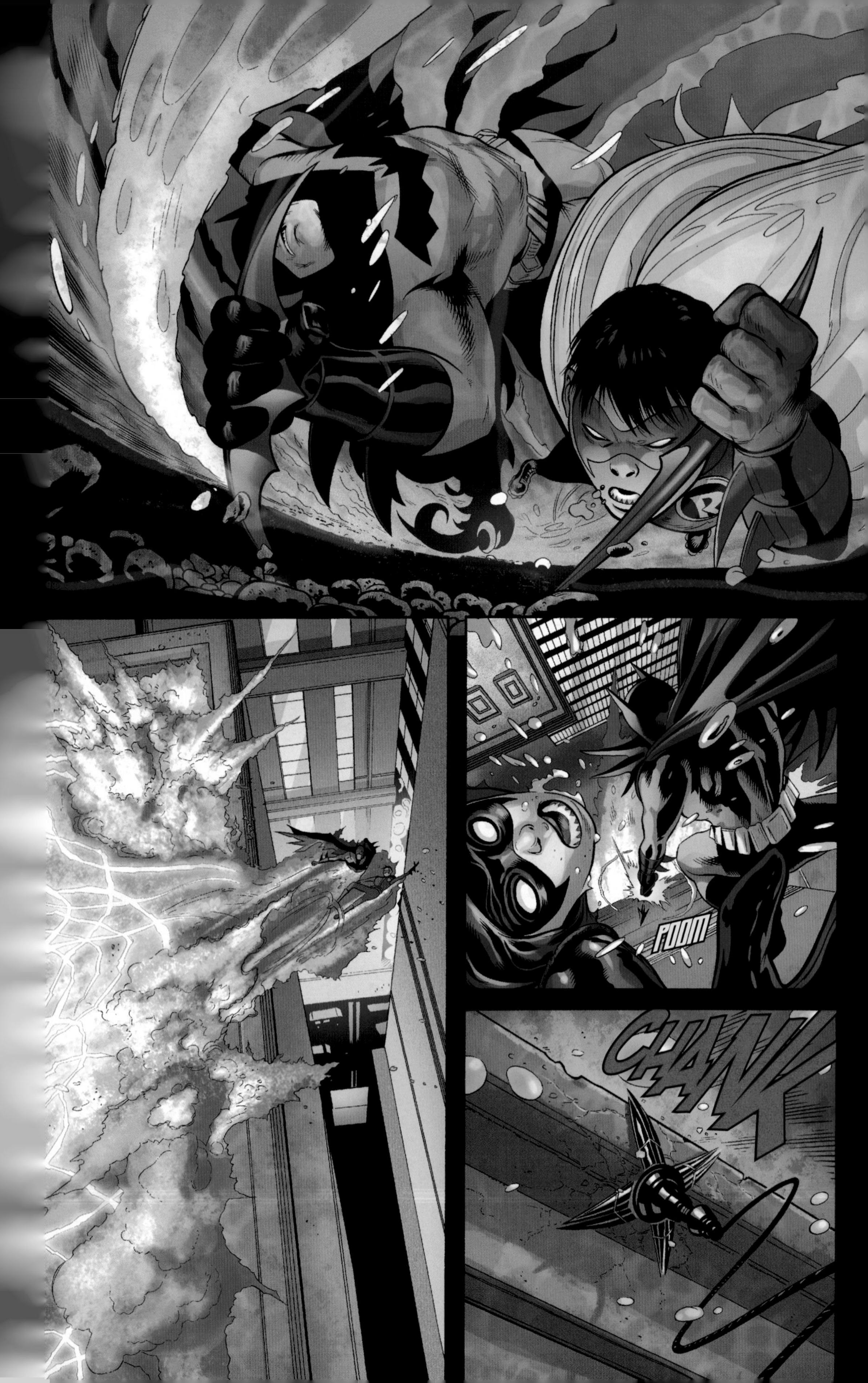
POOM
CHANK

HOLD ON, ROBIN!

YOU'RE THE ONE WHO SHOULD WORRY ABOUT HOLDING ON!

LOOK AT THE PRETTY WATERFALL, MOMMY!

ARE BATMAN AND ROBIN GONNA BE OKAY, MOM?

OF COURSE, AARON. SEE, THEY'RE CLIMBING BACK UP NOW.

DAMMIT, NO SIGN OF HIM...NOT EVEN A RESIDUAL BOOTPRINT.

BUT HE LEFT US PLENTY TO GO ON.

LET'S GET THE LANGSTROMS SQUARED AWAY FIRST.

THE BATBUNKER.

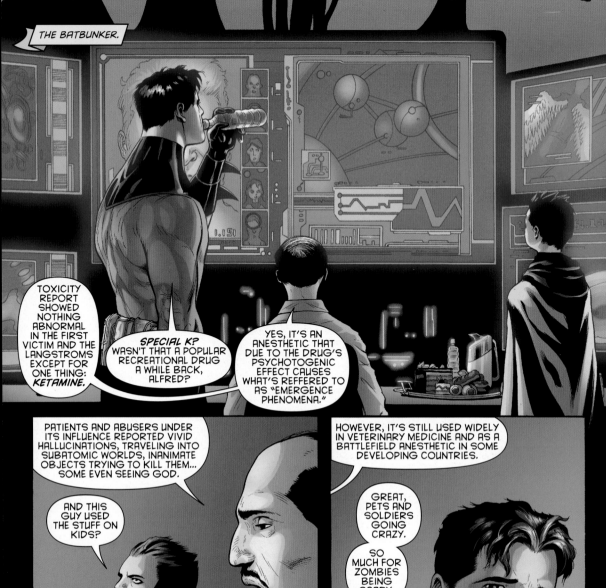

TOXICITY REPORT SHOWED NOTHING ABNORMAL IN THE FIRST VICTIM AND THE LANGSTROMS EXCEPT FOR ONE THING: *KETAMINE.*

SPECIAL K? WASN'T THAT A POPULAR RECREATIONAL DRUG A WHILE BACK, ALFRED?

YES, IT'S AN ANESTHETIC THAT DUE TO THE DRUG'S PSYCHOTOGENIC EFFECT CAUSES WHAT'S REFFERED TO AS "EMERGENCE PHENOMENA."

PATIENTS AND ABUSERS UNDER ITS INFLUENCE REPORTED VIVID HALLUCINATIONS, TRAVELING INTO SUBATOMIC WORLDS, INANIMATE OBJECTS TRYING TO KILL THEM... SOME EVEN SEEING GOD.

AND THIS GUY USED THE STUFF ON KIDS?

I'M GOING TO ENJOY SMASHING THIS WHITE KNIGHT'S FACE WHEN WE FIND HIM.

THE OFFICIAL USE OF KETAMINE'S BEEN REDUCED DRASTICALLY BECAUSE OF THE HIGH POTENTIAL TO CAUSE EMERGENCE PHENOMENA.

HOWEVER, IT'S STILL USED WIDELY IN VETERINARY MEDICINE AND AS A BATTLEFIELD ANESTHETIC IN SOME DEVELOPING COUNTRIES.

GREAT, PETS AND SOLDIERS GOING CRAZY.

SO MUCH FOR ZOMBIES BEING SCARY.

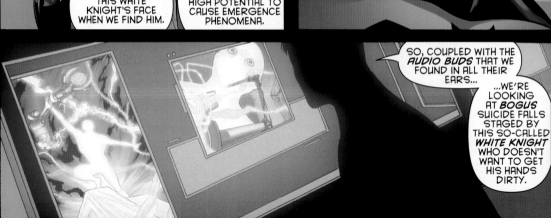

SO, COUPLED WITH THE *AUDIO BUDS* THAT WE FOUND IN ALL THEIR EARS...

...WE'RE LOOKING AT *BOGUS* SUICIDE FALLS STAGED BY THIS SO-CALLED *WHITE KNIGHT* WHO DOESN'T WANT TO GET HIS HANDS DIRTY.

I'VE GIVEN THE WINGS A THOROUGH EXAMINATION. YOU HAVE A VERY PATIENT INDIVIDUAL WHO IS SHOWING GREAT CARE--AND DUE TO THE WORK ON DISPLAY HERE--I'D EVEN HAVE TO SAY *PASSION.*

PASSION?

YEAH, ALFRED'S RIGHT. CHECK OUT THE LAYERING OF THE FEATHERS ACROSS THE WINGSPAN--IT'S PRECISE AND EVEN HAS A COLOR SCHEME TO IT.

LOOK AT THE WAY THE WHITES FADE INTO GREY, JUST LIKE THE FEATHERS OF REAL BIRDS.

HE'S EVEN SIZING THEM PROPERLY, MAKING SURE THE FEATHERS FIT AND MATCH *AERODYNAMICALLY* ALONG WITH A COMPLETE AESTHETIC SENSE.

HE CARES.

HE CARES ABOUT GIVING HIS VICTIMS A PROPER SENDOFF. THE KETAMINE MAKES SURE THEY DON'T FEEL ANY PAIN, AND MAKING SURE THE WINGS ARE PERFECT IN EVERY DETAIL IS HIS WAY OF SHOWING RESPECT FOR THEM...

...LIKE PUTTING THE BEST DRESS OR SUIT ON A CORPSE INSIDE A COFFIN. IT'S IMPORTANT TO THIS *FREAK* THAT HIS VICTIMS HAVE THE ABILITY TO FLY TO HEAVEN AFTER THEY DIE.

YEP, YOU HIT THE NAIL ON THE HEAD. NICE WORK.

YOU HAVE THE MAKINGS OF A FINE DETECTIVE, MASTER DAMIAN.

FAST FORWARD, PENNYWORTH. I'M *ALREADY* A GOOD DETECTIVE.

THEN I'M SURE YOU NOTICED THESE FEATHERS ARE NOT STORE BOUGHT OR SYNTHETIC. SEVERAL SPECIES HAVE BEEN MIXED TO BUILD THESE WINGS.

SEAGULLS, PIGEONS, SPARROWS, EVEN PEREGRINE FALCONS.

⊰tt⊱

PEREGRINE FALCONS? IN THIS CITY? NO WAY.

DO YOU KNOW WHY THERE AREN'T MORE PIGEONS IN GOTHAM?

NO, BUT I'M SURE *YOU'RE* ABOUT TO TELL ME.

PEREGRINE FALCONS ARE RARE IN AN URBAN ENVIRONMENT, BUT THEY'RE AROUND.

COWL OPTIC MAGNIFICATION 150 PERCENT.

PIGEONS ARE EATEN ALIVE AND FED TO THEIR YOUNG. THEIR FEATHERS AND HUSKS ARE USED TO BUILD THE FALCONS' NESTS.

WHAT NESTS?

TWO O'CLOCK. THE APARO APEX BUILDING.

MASK OPTICS UP 150.

FALCONS ARE EPA PROTECTED. THAT'S WHY WE'RE NOT INFESTED WITH PIGEONS LIKE LONDON AND PARIS.

THAT'S SOOOO INCREDIBLY INTERESTING, I CAN'T WAIT TO TWEET IT.

MASK OPTICS 150%

DISTANCE 50 YARDS

AW, ISN'T THAT CUTE...

...A LITTLE DARWINIAN MOMENT.

SNIPERS.

I WAS LEANING MORE TOWARDS ESOTERIC.

THERE'S NOT A LOT OF PEOPLE WHO HAVE ACCESS TO HIGH SKYSCRAPER SPOTS ACROSS THE CITY. WINDOW WASHERS, BUILDING MAINTENANCE GUYS--

YOU KNOW YOUR SENSE OF HUMOR KINDA SUCKS, RIGHT?

WELL I WAS LEANING MORE TOWARDS STUPID.

MASTER RICHARD, WE HAVE A MATCH. THE COMPUTER'S IDENTIFIED OUR FIRST FALLEN ANGEL--

--HIS NAME IS DOUGLAS ZSASZ--

--HE'S THE BROTHER OF VICTOR ZSASZ.

THAT'S THE CONNECTION BETWEEN THE LANGSTROMS AND THE FIRST VICTIM.

THE WHITE KNIGHT'S TARGETS ARE RELATIVES OF ARKHAM'S INMATES!

I'M CONTACTING GORDON IMMEDIATELY, ALFRED, WE NEED TO--

FOOM

FOOM

THAT'S NOT NECESSARY, SIR--

--I BELIEVE HE'S ALREADY CONTACTING YOU.

HAVE NO FEAR, LANGSTROMS...

SNIP

Deceased

FRANCINE LANGSTROM, AARON LANGSTROM, REBECCA LANGSTROM

...I WILL NOT FAIL YOU AGAIN.

YOU WILL NOT BE TAINTED BY YOUR SHADOWED SOULS.

THIS I SWEAR.

BARBARA TETCH, PAUL TETCH, BEN TETCH, SUSAN TETCH

THE TREE NEEDS TO BE REFRESHED FROM TIME TO TIME WITH THE BLOOD OF MARTYRS.

THE SINS OF THE FATHERS AND MOTHERS ARE THE SINS OF YOU ALL.

IT'S NIGHTS LIKE THIS THAT I WISH I HAD A DAMN TEACHING DEGREE.

I GUESS THE WHITE KNIGHT'S IDEA OF *ASCENSION* HAS CHANGED.

THE RANDALLS.

BUT THEY'RE *NOT* RELATED TO ANY OF THE ARKHAM INMATES.

THEY'VE GOT AUDIO BUDS IN THEIR EARS, TOO.

...OKAY, THANKS, SIGLAIN.

THAT WAS GOTHAM MUNICIPAL RECORDS.

WE'RE *NOT* LOOKING AT THE RANDALLS...

...WE'RE LOOKING AT THE *TETCHES.*

AS IN *JERVIS TETCH,* THE MAD HATTER?

YEAH, AND HIS BROTHER AND SISTER.

THE ONE AND ONLY. HIS PARENTS, I ASSUME?

I GUESS JERVIS WAS THE SMALL FRY OF THE FAMILY.

SO THEY CHANGED THEIR NAMES AFTER THEIR SON GREW IN... NOTORIETY.

IT SURE AS HELL DIDN'T HELP.

THEIR SON'S CRAZINESS ENDED UP COMING BACK TO HAUNT--

--THEM.

DO WE HAVE WHAT WE NEED, SERGEANT?

UM, YES, SIR.

THEN CUT THIS FAMILY DOWN BEFORE THE DAMN WIRES SEVER THEIR HANDS AND LEGS!

AND IF THERE'S ANY PRESS LEAKS ABOUT THE DETAILS, SOMEONE'S GONNA FIND THEMSELVES WORKING THE GRAVEYARD SHIFT AT BLACKGATE FOR THE NEXT TEN YEARS!

WE'VE GOT ONE PRIORITY HERE, COMMISSIONER.

WE NEED TO FIND EVERYONE IN GOTHAM WHO WAS RELATED TO ANYONE WHO'S SPENT TIME IN ARKHAM...

"...BEFORE THE WHITE KNIGHT DOES."

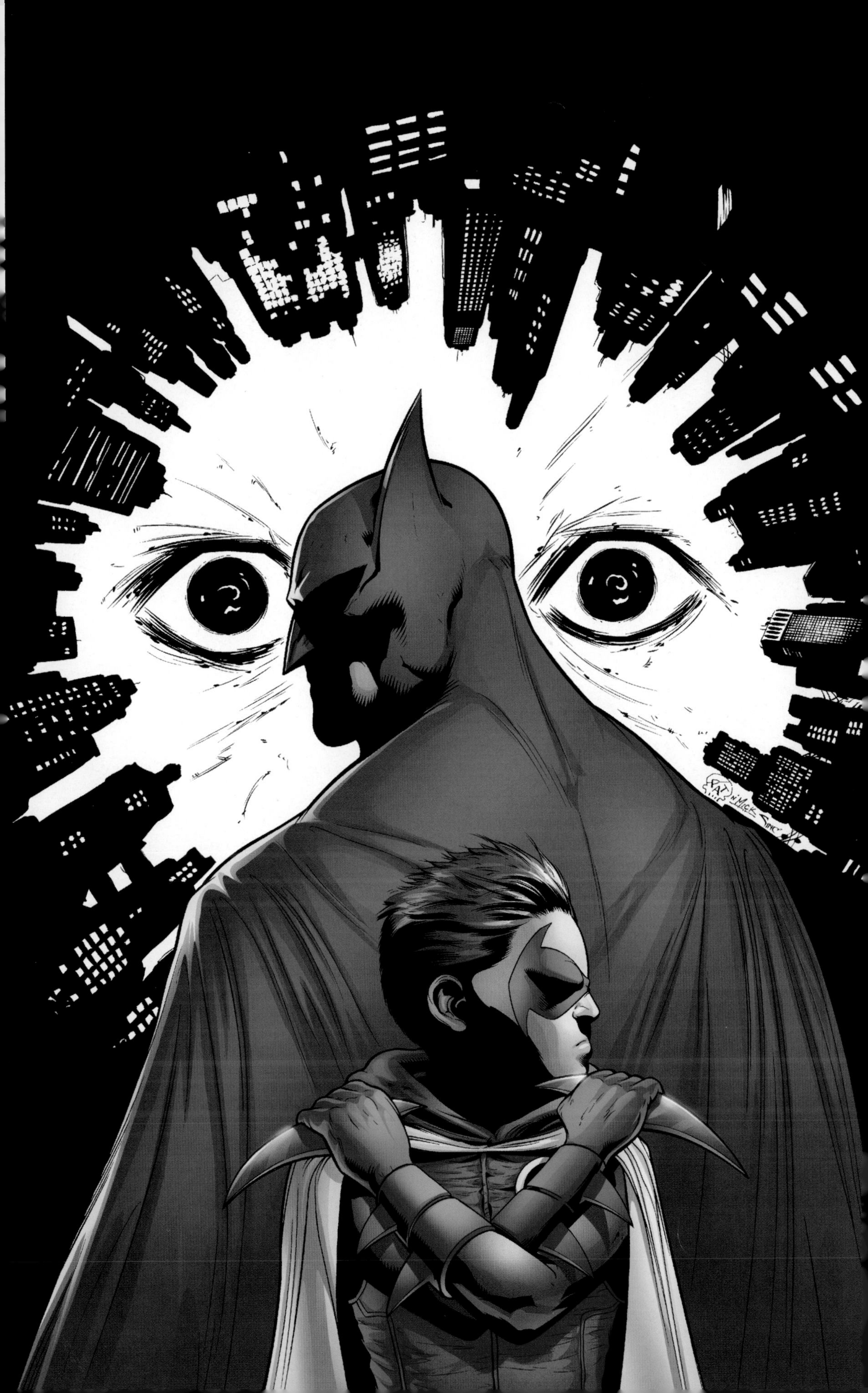

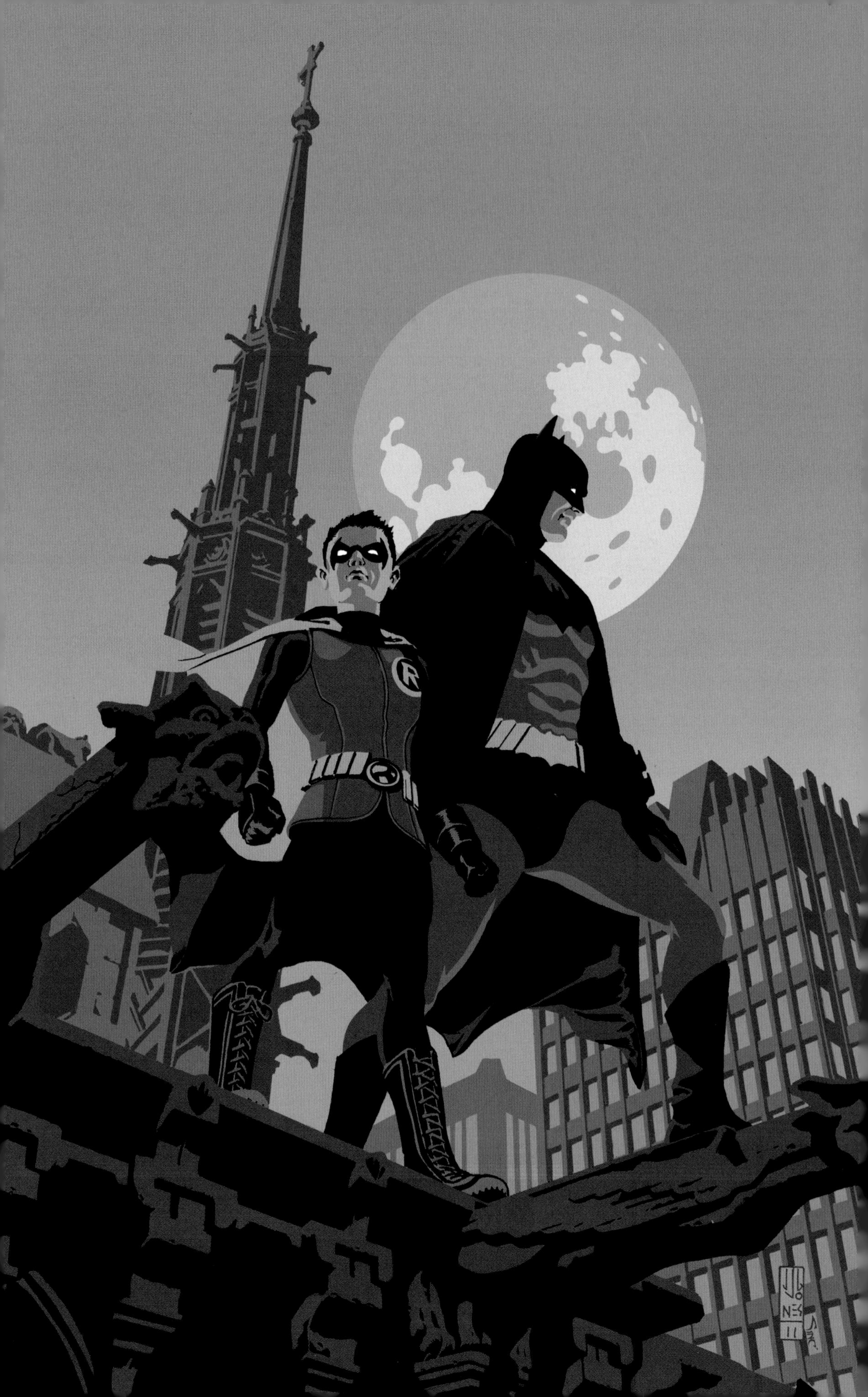

WE NOW SHED OUR SECULAR GARMENTS, ASCENSION HAS BEGUN.

IT'S TIME TO END THE SUFFERING.

YES, IT'S TIME TO END THE SUFFERING.

IT'S GOING ON TWENTY-THREE HOURS! WE'VE COME UP EMPTY, ALFRED, ARE THERE MORE?

SKRFEE

THAT LAST ADDRESS WAS THE FINAL ARKHAM RELATIVE ON THE LIST, BATMAN. GORDON AND HIS MEN HAVE ALSO HAD NO LUCK.

WHERE THE HELL ARE THEY--HOW DID THE WHITE KNIGHT ROUND UP ALL THESE PEOPLE SO FAST?

MAYBE HE DIDN'T HAVE TO, ROBIN--MAYBE HE HAD THEM ALREADY.

ALFRED, HAVE YOU DECIPHERED THE FREQUENCY OSCILLATION FROM THE PREVIOUS VICTIM'S EAR TRANSMITTERS?

YES, AND OUR SATELLITES WILL BE ONLINE AND READY TO DISRUPT ALL CITYWIDE SIGNALS IN THIRTY

I WILL NOT ADD TO THE WORLD'S PAIN.

ANGELS ARE FALLING ON GOTHAM!

Tree of Blood

DARK KNIGHT VS. WHITE KNIGHT
CONCLUSION

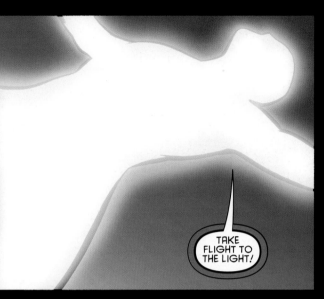

TAKE FLIGHT TO THE LIGHT!

ACTIVATE THE JAMMING DEVICE, ALFRED-- NOW!

PETER J. TOMASI: WRITER   **PATRICK GLEASON:** PENCILLER

MICK GRAY: INKER ADDITIONAL INKS BY **KEITH CHAMPAGNE** AND **TOM NGUYEN**
ALEX SINCLAIR: COLORIST   **PATRICK BROSSEAU:** LETTERER   **GLEASON, GRAY, SINCLAIR:** COVER

SIGNAL DISRUPTION IN PROGRESS, BATMAN.

ANYONE WEARING THOSE EAR TRANSMITTERS WITHIN GOTHAM'S CITY LIMITS...

"...WILL BE IN EXTREME PAIN..."

"...FOLLOWED BY SUDDEN UNCONSCIOUSNESS."

HARNESS! WE'RE GOING FOR A RIDE!

I'M SET! PUNCH IT!

THERE'S TOO MANY OF THEM!

WE CAN'T SAVE EVERYONE!

FWOOSH

POOM

POOM

POOM

WE SAVE WHO WE CAN!

AND THEN WE MAKE SURE WHOEVER DID THIS--

--PAYS FOR IT!

SPEED LIMIT 30

EACH AND EVERY WING-WEARING ANGEL WAS CONNECTED BY BLOOD OR MARRIAGE TO SOMEONE WHO'S SERVED TIME BEHIND *ARKHAM'S* WALLS.

THIS WHITE KNIGHT IS THINKING THE APPLE *DOESN'T* FALL FAR FROM THE TREE.

SOMETIMES IT DOES, SOMETIMES IT DOESN'T.

THAT A SHOT AT ME? BECAUSE I'M SURE EVERYONE IN THE GREEN AND GLOWING *GRAYSON* FAMILY TREE WASN'T ALL SMILING SAVANT DO-GOODERS...

DIDN'T KNOW YOU WERE SO SENSITIVE.

MAYBE I SHOULD SEE HOW *SENSITIVE* YOUR LOWER VERTEBRAE ARE.

WE'RE TALKING *NATURE VERSUS NURTURE* HERE-- AND BY THE LOOKS OF IT, THIS GUY'S ON THE *NATURE* SIDE.

YEAH, AND WHAT SIDE ARE *YOU* ON?

NEITHER SIDE. ALL OF US PICK A ROAD--LOOK AT WHAT YOU DID A FEW WEEKS AGO--YOU TURNED YOUR BACK ON YOUR OWN *MOTHER.*

YOU TURNED AWAY FROM *EVIL*--YOU DIDN'T EMBRACE THE *AL GHUL* PLAYBOOK EVEN THOUGH IT WAS EASIER--EVEN THOUGH IT WAS IN *YOUR BLOOD.*

YOU MADE A CHOICE TO *HELP*, DAMIAN, TO MAKE A DIFFERENCE, WHICH IS *ALWAYS HARDER.*

IF I MAY, WE GO TO SOMEONE'S AID BECAUSE WE WANT TO, BECAUSE WE NEED TO, AND *THAT* IS WHAT DEFINES US--

--THAT IS WHAT DEFINES *YOU*, MASTER DAMIAN, NOT THAT YOUR MOTHER IS TALIA AL GHUL AND YOUR FATHER IS BRUCE WAYNE.

IN THE END, *YOU MAKE YOU*. NO ONE ELSE.

EXPECTING A BIRTHDAY GIFT FROM ME THIS YEAR OR SOMETHING?

GOT IT, PENNYWORTH. *I'M* THE BOSS OF ME. THANKS.

OKAY, THESE ANGELS-- THEY'RE RELATED TO KILLERS AND SLIME, BUT *NONE* OF THEM HAD A RAP SHEET--TRAFFIC VIDS AND A FEW MISDEMEANORS, SURE. BUT THAT'S IT, SO WHY?

WHAT IF THE WHITE KNIGHT'S GETTING TO THEM *BEFORE THEY GO DARK*--BEFORE THEY TURN INTO SOMETHING...

INTO WHAT, RICHARD?

INTO WHATEVER *TURNS* SOMEONE INTO AN INMATE OF ARKHAM.

THINK ABOUT THE NOTE WE FOUND AND WHAT BYSTANDERS HEARD THE ANGELS SAYING: "IT'S TIME TO END THE SUFFERING. I WILL NOT ADD TO THE WORLD'S PAIN."

SO THE WHITE KNIGHT'S *SUBTRACTING*-- LOOKING AT THE INMATES AS PEOPLE WHO'VE *SPREAD PAIN.*

IN HIS MIND THEY'RE ALL *TAINTED* WITH BAD BLOOD--THEY'RE TICKING HUMAN BOMBS--AND IF NOT THIS GENERATION MAYBE THE NEXT, OR THE ONE AFTER THAT.

HIS PLAN BOILS DOWN TO TWO WORDS: *PREEMPTIVE STRIKE.*

AGAINST THESE ANGELS BEFORE THEY POSSIBLY KILL SOMEONE.

HE WANTS THEIR *BLOODLINES* STOPPED HERE AND NOW.

AGAINST WHAT?

I'M AFRAID THIS WHITE KNIGHT MAY HAVE JUST TURNED HIS ATTENTION TO THE *SOURCE.*

ARKHAM'S LIT UP LIKE A *CHRISTMAS TREE.*

GCN BREAKING NEWS

ARKHAM ASYLUM

SWAT

LOOKS LIKE THEY PUT IN A FEW MORE NIGHTLIGHTS SINCE OUR LAST VISIT.

C-CAN'T SEE--

MY EYES--

NO MATTER WHAT--KEEP YOUR WEAPONS HOLSTERED AND SLUNG!

VRRRROOM

THAT SOUND-- NO OTHER ENGINE SOUNDS LIKE--

COMMISSIONER!

BATMAN! THANK GOD!

ALL OF YOU-- SIT DOWN WHERE YOU ARE AND DON'T MOVE UNTIL BACKUP ARRIVES!

THE MORE YOU STUMBLE AROUND, THE MORE PANIC AND CONFUSION YOU'RE GOING TO CAUSE!

WHAT HAPPENED?

THAT'S GOOD TO HEAR, BATMAN, BECAUSE I'D HATE TO LIVE THE REST OF MY LIFE IN THE DARK.

YOU AND ME BOTH, COMMISSIONER.

SPOTTED A BIRD-LIKE CREATURE LANDING ON THE ARKHAM ROOF RIGHT BEFORE WE COULD MAKE OUR WAY IN-- BRIGHT STICKS-- LIKE ARROWS-- CAME OUT OF NOWHERE AND BURST INTO INTENSE FLASHES--

--BLINDING ALL OF US--

BOTH YOUR PUPILS JUST CONSTRICTED AND DILATED SLIGHTLY-- I THINK IT'S ONLY TEMPORARY.

YOUR REDEEMER IS HERE!

⇒YAGHH!⇐

⇒NGGHH!⇐

YOU MAY NOT RECOGNIZE SOME OF THEM, BUT YOU'RE ALL *KIN*--RELATED TO EACH AND EVERY ANGEL IN THESE PICTURES.

--THAT YOU'VE ALREADY LET RULE *YOUR* SINISTER SOULS.

DROWNING IS NOT MY FORTE.

RRAGHH!

YOU'RE THE EXCEPTION, MISTER JOKER...

YES, I *ALWAYS* AM.

...I *COULDN'T* FIND ANY FAMILY TIES WHATSOEVER TO YOU.

THAT'S BECAUSE I'VE *CUT* THEM ALREADY.

MOTHERS, FATHERS, BROTHERS, SISTERS, AUNTS, UNCLES, COUSINS...

...YOU ALL COME FROM THE SAME *TREE OF BLOOD.*

I'VE GIVEN THEM *WINGS* AND STOPPED THEM FOREVER FROM EMBRACING THE EVIL--

YOUR *EYES* ARE AS MESMERIZING AS YOUR LIGHT. I WOULD LOVE TO *WEAR* YOUR FACE.

NOBODY GETS TO KILL MY FAMILY BUT ME.

HELLO, DOCTOR PHOSPHORUS.

THAT'S MY AUNT NANCY'S FAMILY IN THAT PICTURE...

YES, YOUR MOTHER'S SISTER.

YOU KILLED THEM!

NO, I *FREED* THEM.

I'M SURE YOU DON'T REMEMBER ME, BUT I DO REMEMBER *YOU.*

"THAT'S BECAUSE I WAS JUST A BOY...

WHAT'RE YOU TALKING ABOUT? I'VE NEVER SEEN YOU BEFORE IN MY LIFE.

"...A BOY WHO HAD TO GO TO WORK WITH HIS FATHER ONE DAY BECAUSE HIS MOTHER WAS GONE AND HIS FATHER DIDN'T HAVE ANY SICK DAYS LEFT.

"IT WAS AGAINST THE RULES TO HAVE ANY VISITORS, BUT MY FATHER'S FRIENDS ALWAYS HELPED EACH OTHER OUT.

"...UNTIL ALL THE TV'S SUDDENLY ENDED UP PLAYING THE *SAME SHOW.*

"THAT SHOW WAS A *RIOT*--A RIOT MY FATHER TRIED TO STOP...

"...BUT INSTEAD IT *STOPPED HIM.*

"I GOT TO READ COMICS AND WATCH TV ALL DAY...

"YOU GAVE MY FATHER *WINGS*--WINGS TO FLY AWAY FROM THIS WORLD BEFORE HE COULD BE CORRUPTED AND INFECTED BY IT.

"HE FLEW INTO THE LIGHT THAT DAY..."

...AND NOW I'M HERE TO *PURIFY* YOUR BLACK HEARTS AND MAKE SURE YOU *ALL* FLY INTO THE LIGHT, TOO.

MY CRUSADE HAS *JUST BEGUN.* I'M NOT ONLY GOING TO SAVE GOTHAM, I'M GOING TO SAVE THIS COUNTRY AND THEN THE *WORLD.*

I'VE GOT A BETTER IDEA--

--HOW ABOUT JUST SAVING YOUR BREATH INSTEAD?!

UGGN

ZRAKK

DO YOU REALLY THINK I'D LET--

--A CREATURE OF THE NIGHT STOP ME?!

YOU STOLE THEIR LIVES FROM ME!

THOSE WERE MY MARKS TO CARVE--NOT YOURS!

>UFFF<

ZZRAP

ARGHH

SHUNK

SHUNK

FAAASSSHH

>ARRGH< I DON'T NEED TO SEE YOU, BOY TO BLEED YOU!

THESE OPAQUE OPTIC FILTERS I DESIGNED CAME IN HANDY.

PUT ZSASZ DOWN AND FIND A WAY TO SHUT THE LIQUID OFF--

--WE CAN'T LET THESE PSYCHOS OUT BUT WE CAN'T LET THEM DROWN EITHER!

ZZRAP

ZZRAP

POOM

THAT'S FOR ALL THE KIDS YOU PUT THROUGH HELL A FEW WEEKS BACK, ZSASZ!

K-KAFF-K

AND HEY, IS IT JUST YOU--

--OR CAN *ANYBODY* SIGN IN?!

SHRRIP

ARGHHH

BAKOOM!

UGNNN

WHAT'RE YOU WAITING FOR--YOU JUST GOING TO LET US DROWN?!

I'M NOT SUPPOSED TO DIE ON MY BIRTHDAY!

HOLD ON A SECOND, I'M THINKING...

YOU SHOULD BE FIGHTING BESIDE ME, NOT *AGAINST* ME, BATMAN!

BUT INSTEAD YOU EMBRACE DARKNESS, AND WE BOTH KNOW THAT DARKNESS *BEGETS* DARKNESS.

YOU'RE WRONG! I *USE* DARKNESS TO SHINE A LIGHT--WHILE YOU USE LIGHT TO MURDER *INNOCENT* MEN, WOMEN AND CHILDREN!

THE *TAINTED* CAN'T STAY INNOCENT FOR *LONG*, BATMAN.

KLIK

ARRGH!

FWOOSH

FWOOSH

SHUNK

SHADOWS NEED TO BLEED TO *EXPOSE* THE LUMINOSITY UNDERNEATH!

UNNN

SOMETIMES SYMBOLS OF DARKNESS NEED TO BE *ERADICATED* TO GIVE PEOPLE HOPE, BATMAN.

FOOM

AND SOMETIMES DELUSIONAL IDIOTS NEED TO SHUT THE HELL UP!

AARRGH!

I KNEW MY PATH WOULD BE FILLED WITH PAIN!

I HAVE ALWAYS ACCEPTED THAT!

I DON'T THINK SO!

ONCE MY ARCLIGHT TRANSFORMS ARKHAM, PEOPLE WILL LOOK UP AND SEE A SHINING BEACON ON A HILL AND REMEMBER IT WAS THE FIRST STEP TO A *BRIGHT NEW WORLD!*

NO! THERE'S STILL SO MUCH I NEED TO--

KRAKK

DID YOU SAVE THOSE *RATS* FROM DROWNING?

UNFORTUNATELY, YES.

ARE THOSE *YOUR* COWL EARS STICKING IN HIS HEAD?

YEP.

≥TT≤

YOU'RE MEANER THAN I THOUGHT.

I LIKE IT.

LOOK AT THIS GUY...WRONG PLACE AT THE WRONG TIME AS A KID--BLOWS A GASKET-- ENDS UP IN HERE SURROUNDED BY THE SAME WACKOS HE WAS TRYING TO KILL FOR MURDERING HIS FATHER...

...WHAT A COSMIC CRAP SHOOT.

ANY WORD ON HIS SKIN AND FEATURES, BATMAN?

COUPLED WITH THE BLAST AND THE UNIDENTIFIABLE SERUM ORIGINALLY INGESTED, HIS CONDITION'S PERMANENT. THE WINGS--PROGNOSIS?

FUSED TO HIS BODY AFTER THAT WEAPON OF HIS EXPLODED. THE TECH BOYS ARE STILL TRYING TO FIGURE OUT WHAT WAS LEFT OF IT.

LEWIS BAYARD'S GONE FROM BEING A WHITE KNIGHT TO A WHITE ANGEL.

MAYBE HAVING AN ANGEL IN THE NEXT CELL WILL GET THE INMATES TO THE PRISON CHAPEL MORE ON SUNDAYS.

I DOUBT THAT.

AWRIGHT, LIGHTS OUT!

END

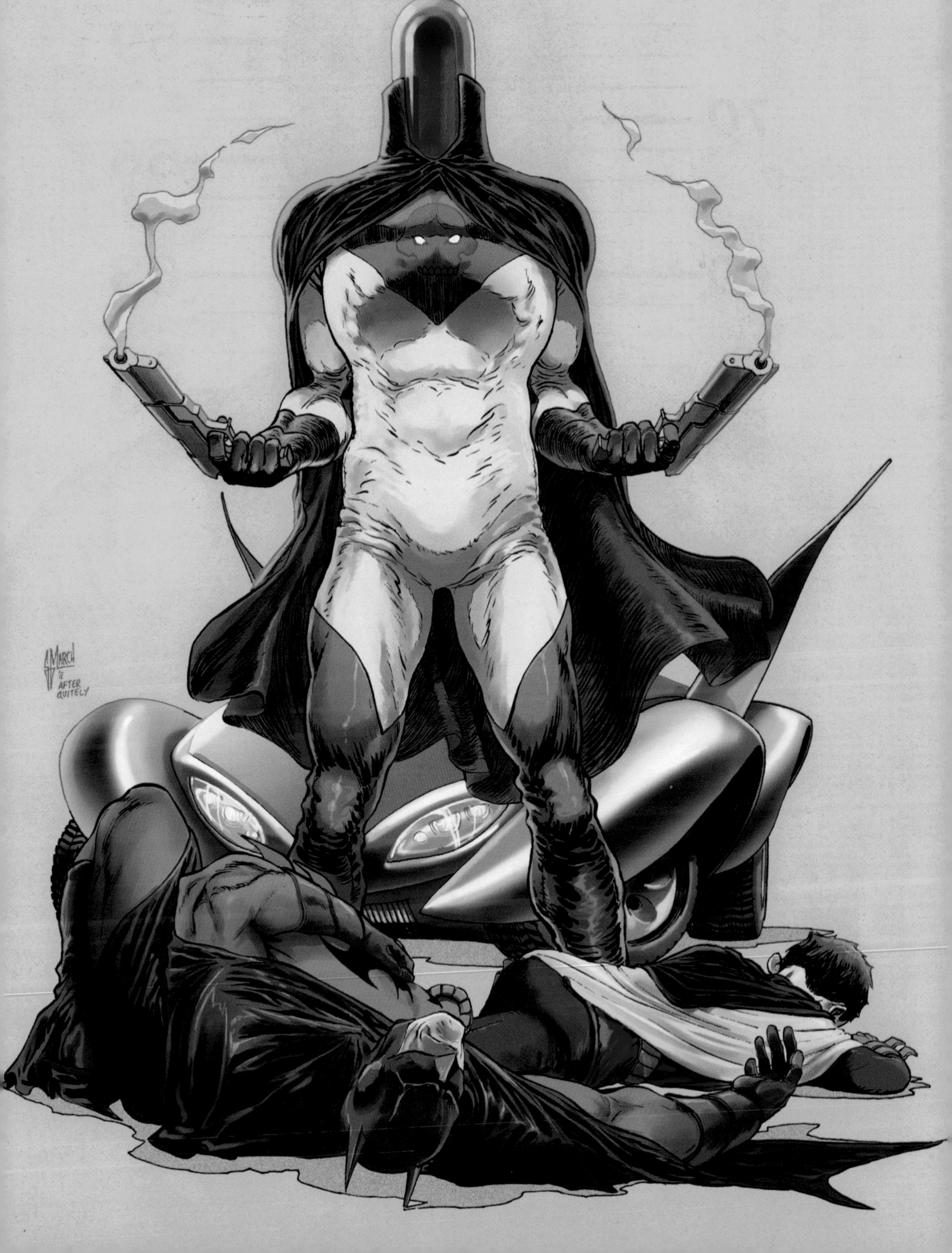
MARCH
AFTER
QUITELY

8081N02
TODD, JASON
GOTHAM DEPT.
CORRECTIONS

YEARS AGO AND LIFETIMES AWAY.

"HE'S GOOD."

"HE WILL BE."

"A BIT ROUGH AROUND THE EDGES."

"A BIT *BRAZEN.* A BIT OVERCONFIDENT.

"AND DON'T GET ME WRONG, BRUCE, THIS ISN'T ABOUT HIS BACKGROUND. IT'S NOT BECAUSE HE'S *A STREET KID.*"

"CONFIDENCE IS GOOD. RESTRAINT CAN BE TAUGHT. YOU KNOW THAT AS WELL AS *ANYONE,* DICK.

"HE HAS A *LOT* TO LEARN. BUT I WOULDN'T HAVE BROUGHT HIM OUT IF HE WASN'T READY."

"I AGREE-- HE'S READY.

"BUT THAT'S JUST *NOW.* THIS ISN'T A SHORT-TERM OCCUPATION. GROWING UP AT YOUR KNEE ISN'T EASY."

"I AM ABUNDANTLY AWARE OF THAT..."

...I KNOW HE'S NOT *YOU.*

THAT ISN'T MY CONCERN OR FOCUS.

NO, HE'S NOT. MAYBE HE'LL BE *BETTER* THAN ME.

"HE'S *ROBIN.*"

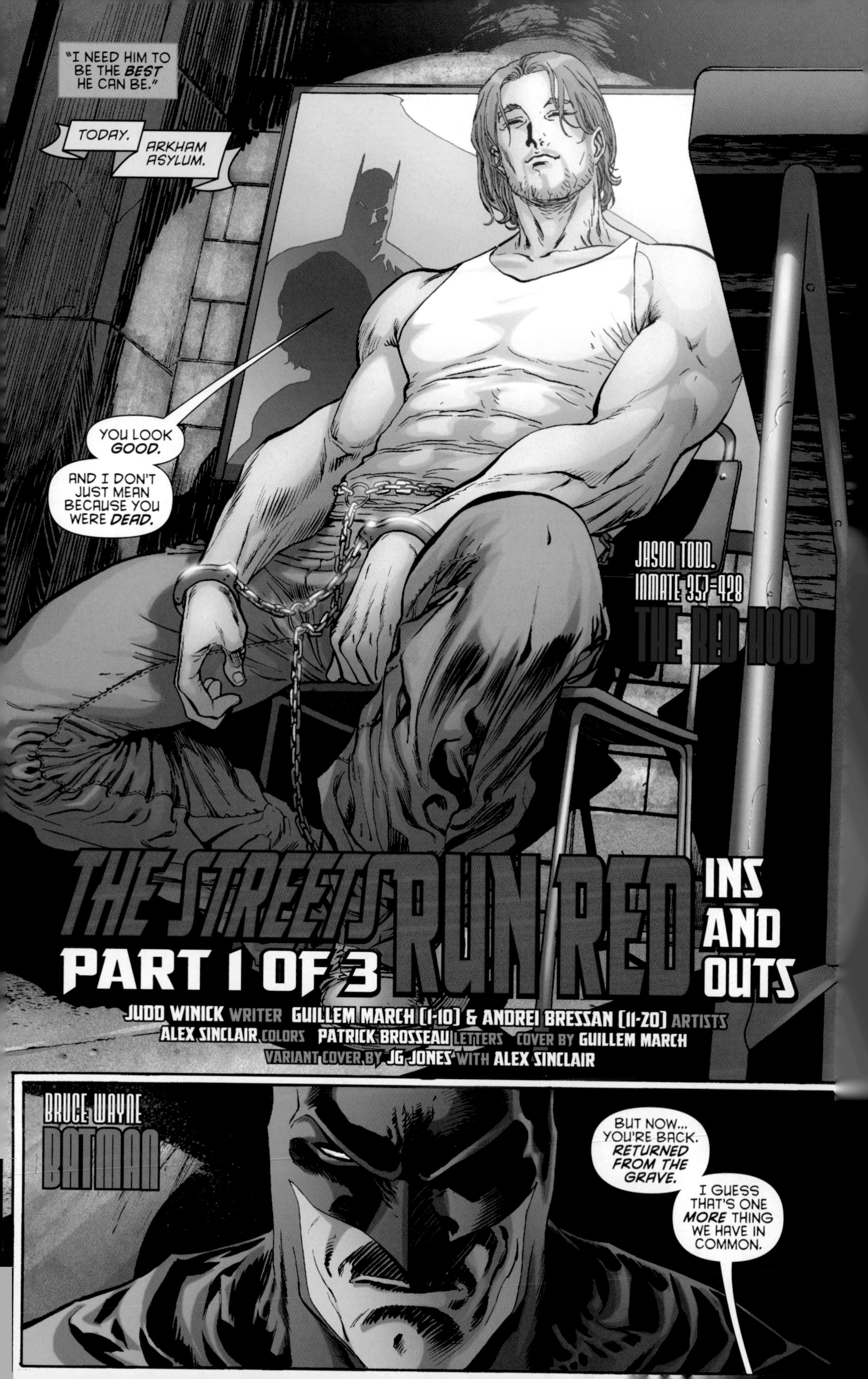
"I NEED HIM TO BE THE BEST HE CAN BE."
TODAY.
ARKHAM ASYLUM.
YOU LOOK GOOD.
AND I DON'T JUST MEAN BECAUSE YOU WERE DEAD.
JASON TODD.
INMATE 357-428
THE RED HOOD
THE STREETS RUN RED
PART 1 OF 3
INS AND OUTS
JUDD WINICK WRITER GUILLEM MARCH [1-10] & ANDREI BRESSAN [11-20] ARTISTS
ALEX SINCLAIR COLORS PATRICK BROSSEAU LETTERS COVER BY GUILLEM MARCH
VARIANT COVER BY JG JONES WITH ALEX SINCLAIR
BRUCE WAYNE
BATMAN
BUT NOW... YOU'RE BACK. RETURNED FROM THE GRAVE.
I GUESS THAT'S ONE MORE THING WE HAVE IN COMMON.

In here they just know him as the Red Hood.

I KNEW YOU WEREN'T *REALLY* CROAKED. NOT *YOU*. NOT LIKE THAT.

DARKSEID FRIES YOU WITH HIS *OMEGA EFFECT?* PLEASE. TOO MUCH *METAPHYSICAL* HORSE CRAP.

And he hasn't told the authorities his *real* name.

He has no identity. There's no record of his fingerprints *anywhere* on Earth. Like *me*. Like *Dick*. Like *Tim*. Like *Damian*.

HOW WAS *YOUR* TRIP BACK? I MEAN, FROM THE *GREAT BEYOND* AND BACK TO THE LAND OF THE *LIVING?*

ME, I WAS ALWAYS *FUZZY* ON THE DETAILS OF MY LITTLE *JOURNEY*. IT COMES IN *FLASHES*. DRIPS. DRABS.

To say the very least, if anyone knew he was *Bruce Wayne's* late ward *Jason Todd*...that would spark way too many questions.

I *MOSTLY* REMEMBER BEING BRAIN DAMAGED.

CLAWING MY WAY OUT OF A *COFFIN*.

WITH MY *BARE* HANDS.

Questions from outsiders is *not* what Jason wants.

This is between us.

A family matter.

GEEZ, BUT LISTEN TO ME GOING ON AND ON. SORRY, I'M A BIT *"LIMITED"* WHEN IT COMES TO VISITORS, BUT TELL ME...

...*HOW ARE YOU?*

YOU PETITIONED THE COURTS FOR A TRANSFER FROM *ARKHAM* TO ANOTHER CORRECTIONAL FACILITY.

REALLY? AFTER *EVERYTHING* WE'VE BEEN THROUGH WE'RE JUST GOING TO SKIP TO *"BUSINESS"*?

C'MON, THROW A DUDE A BONE. A LITTLE SMALL TALK. HOW'S *DAMIAN'S MOM?*

YOU'RE IN *ARKHAM* FOR YOUR *SAFETY.*

THAT'S NOT LEGAL. THIS IS A *NUT HOUSE.* I AM NOT CRAZY. I MURDERED *CRIMINALS.*

GRANTED, I GOT DRESSED UP IN A GOOFY OUTFIT TO DO IT, BUT LOOK IN A MIRROR, *NOSFERATU*--THAT DOESN'T GET ME THE RUBBER ROOM.

I HAVE PASSED *ALL* OF MY *PSYCH EXAMS*--MULTIPLE TIMES. I AM SIMPLY *HOMICIDAL.* WILL I KILL AGAIN? *SURE.* AM I BAD PERSON? OH YEAH.

SO KEEP ME LOCKED UP. JUST NOT *HERE.*

I WILL *NOT* BE HOUSED IN YOUR *KENNEL* FOR *FREAKS.*

"HE WON'T BE *SAFE* IN A CONVENTIONAL PRISON..."

DICK GRAYSON
BATMAN

TODD, JASON

...THERE WILL BE A LIST OF ENEMIES A *MILE* LONG LOCKED UP IN THERE WITH HIM. UNLESS HE'S IN TWENTY-FOUR-HOUR *PROTECTIVE CUSTODY*, ALL HE'LL BE DOING IS FENDING OFF *ATTACKS.*

WHY WOULD HE PUT HIMSELF AT SUCH *RISK?*

DAMIAN WAYNE
ROBIN

HE'S *PLANNING* SOMETHING. YES, HE'S UNSTABLE...UNPREDICTABLE... BUT CONFINED TO ARKHAM, HE'S HAD LITTLE ELSE TO DO BUT *THINK.*

YOU NEED TO BE PREPARED.

BECAUSE HE'S *PSYCHOTIC.*

IT'S NOT THAT SIMPLE.

WE'LL KEEP AN EYE ON HIM.

THAT'S *NOT* WHAT I'M SAYING. I BELIEVE THAT BY THE TIME YOU HAVE *ANY* SENSE OF WHAT HE'S UP TO...

"...IT WILL BE *TOO LATE.*"

GOTHAM CITY CORRECTIONS.

HEY, *RED.*

OR SHOULD I CALL YOU *MR. HOOD?* CUZ I AM LOOKING AT *THE RED HOOD*, RIGHT?

YOU'RE LOOKIN' AT HIM.

LOOKING AT A MAN WHOZE IN FOR SOME *TROUBLE.*

MARTIN *"THE BEAVER"* LITTLEMAN...

...I KILLED YOUR *BROTHER*, RIGHT? HIM AND ABOUT THIRTEEN OTHER *MORONS* WHO WORKED FOR HIM.

I'D SAY I WAS *SORRY*, BUT I THINK WE *BOTH* KNOW I WOULDN'T *REALLY* MEAN IT.

YOU'RE *DEAD.* YOU HEAR ME?

I HATE TO TELL YA, BEAV...

"...DEATH DIDN'T DO *ANYTHING* EXCEPT SLOW ME DOWN A LITTLE."

YO, *BEAVER.* YOU WANTED TO TALK TO THAT WILMA DUDE ABOUT MORE PRODUCT?

BEAVER-- WE GOTTA *JET.* HE CAN'T BE TALKING TO YOU FOR TOO LONG OR--

BEAV?

GUARD!

YOU *SURE* YOU WANT TO BE DOING THIS *YOURSELF,* BOSS?

Pride & Prejudice

I'M *SURE.* WE GOOD?

GOOD.

LET'S HIT IT.

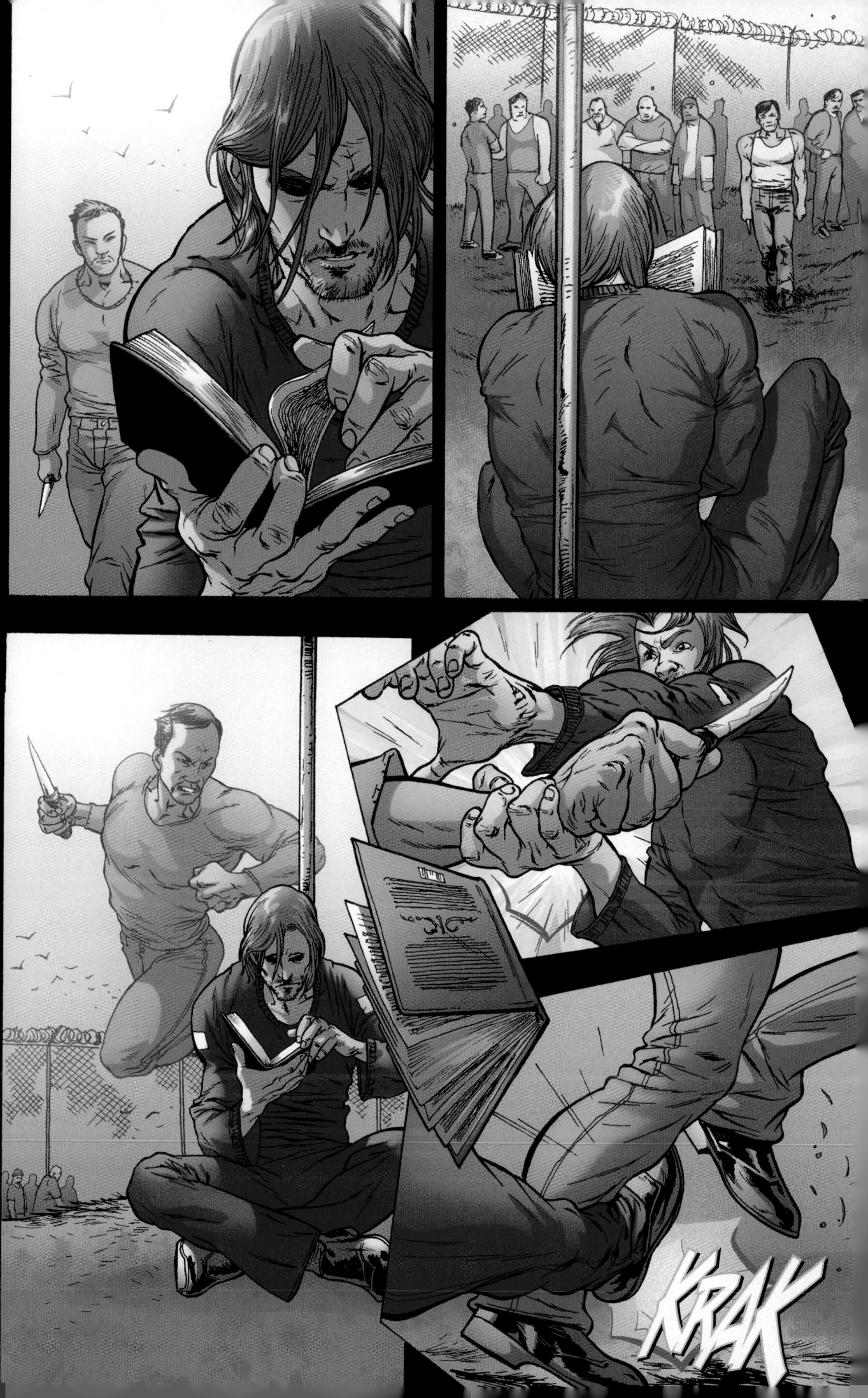
KRAK

KRUNK!

DOWN! EVERYBODY GET DOWN!

THAT'S HIM.

--KILL THAT SON OF A--

--DO IT FAST--

--MONEY ON HIS HEAD--

--WALKING PAY DAY--

This crew is called *"Little Doubt."* And they're from out of town.

WHY ARE YOU IN GOTHAM?

WE'RE TAKING IN A SHOW.

BUT *THEATER* IN THIS BURG REALLY *SUCKS.*

LET ME HIT THEM SOME MORE.

YOU'VE GOT A TRUCE WITH THE *COLLINGWOOD GANG.* YOU DON'T *EVER* COME THIS FAR NORTH.

YOU NEED TO KEEP UP ON *CURRENT EVENTS,* BATS.

THERE AIN'T NO MORE *COLLINGWOOD GANG.*

"BEAVER LITTLEMAN OFFED HIMSELF IN THE CAN."

I *INSTRUCTED* YOU TO NOTIFY ME IF *ANYTHING* UNUSUAL HAPPENED, WARDEN!

I DIDN'T SEE IT AS *UNUSUAL*-- NOT AT FIRST!

NINE *SUICIDES*, AND *SIX-MURDERS* OF HIGH-RANKING CRIMINALS DIDN'T SEEM *UNUSUAL?!*

NO! WELL--*YES!* BUT I DIDN'T THINK WE HAD ANY REASON TO SUSPECT *THE RED HOOD*--UNTIL NOW!

WHY--WHAT HAPPENED *NOW?*

"82 ARE *DEAD*.

"OVER A HUNDRED ARE ILL. WE THINK IT WAS IN THE FOOD.

"*POISON* IN THE FOOD."

IDIOTS.

DON'T DO *ANYTHING*, I'M EN ROUTE.

DO NOT MOVE HIM! PUT HIM IN ISOLATION UNTIL I ARRIVE!

FORGET IT. HE'S *OUT* OF MY PRISON. HE'S GOING BACK TO ARKHAM.

YOU'RE TOO LATE.

"HE'S ALREADY ON HIS WAY."

I like trouble.

I can't help it.

I've always been this way.

It made me a juvie.

A teenage vigilante.

Got me killed.

It had me putting on a helmet and murdering criminals.

So, it's not like my behavior is a big secret.

So, you put me in a building with 14,000 dirtbags who deserve nothing more than a hot shot and a trip to the morgue--

--and you think I'm going to behave myself? Well, hell, you just haven't been paying attention.

So, now it's back to Arkham.

Unless something else should come up...

TRANSPORT 31--WE'VE BEEN HIT! WE'RE HIT! MAN DOWN! LEAD CAR HAS BEEN--!

GA-KOOOM!!!

ON YOUR FEET!

GET ON THE DAMN RADIO! WE NEED BACK-UP! NOW!

WAIT! YOU HEAR THAT?! SOMETHING'S ON THE--

GRDOONK!

ACK-ACK-ACK-ACK-ACK-ACK-ACK-ACK-ACK-

ACK-ACK-ACK-ACK-ACK-ACK-ACK-ACK-ACK-

ACK-ACK-ACK-ACK-ACK-ACK-

AND WHO THE HELL ARE YOU GUYS?

WE'RE THE ONES WHO'RE BREAKING YOU OUT OF PRISON.

WORKS FOR ME.

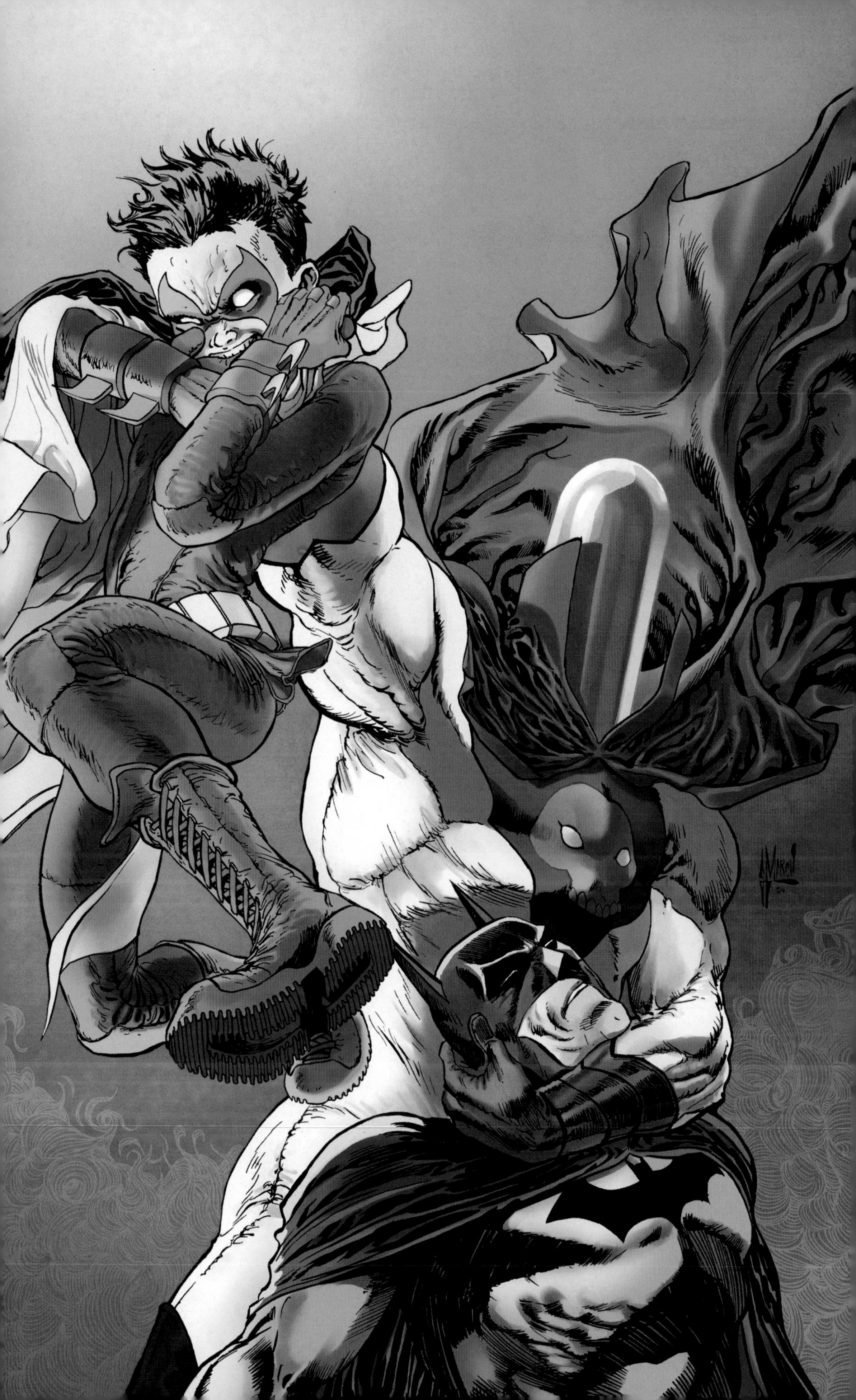

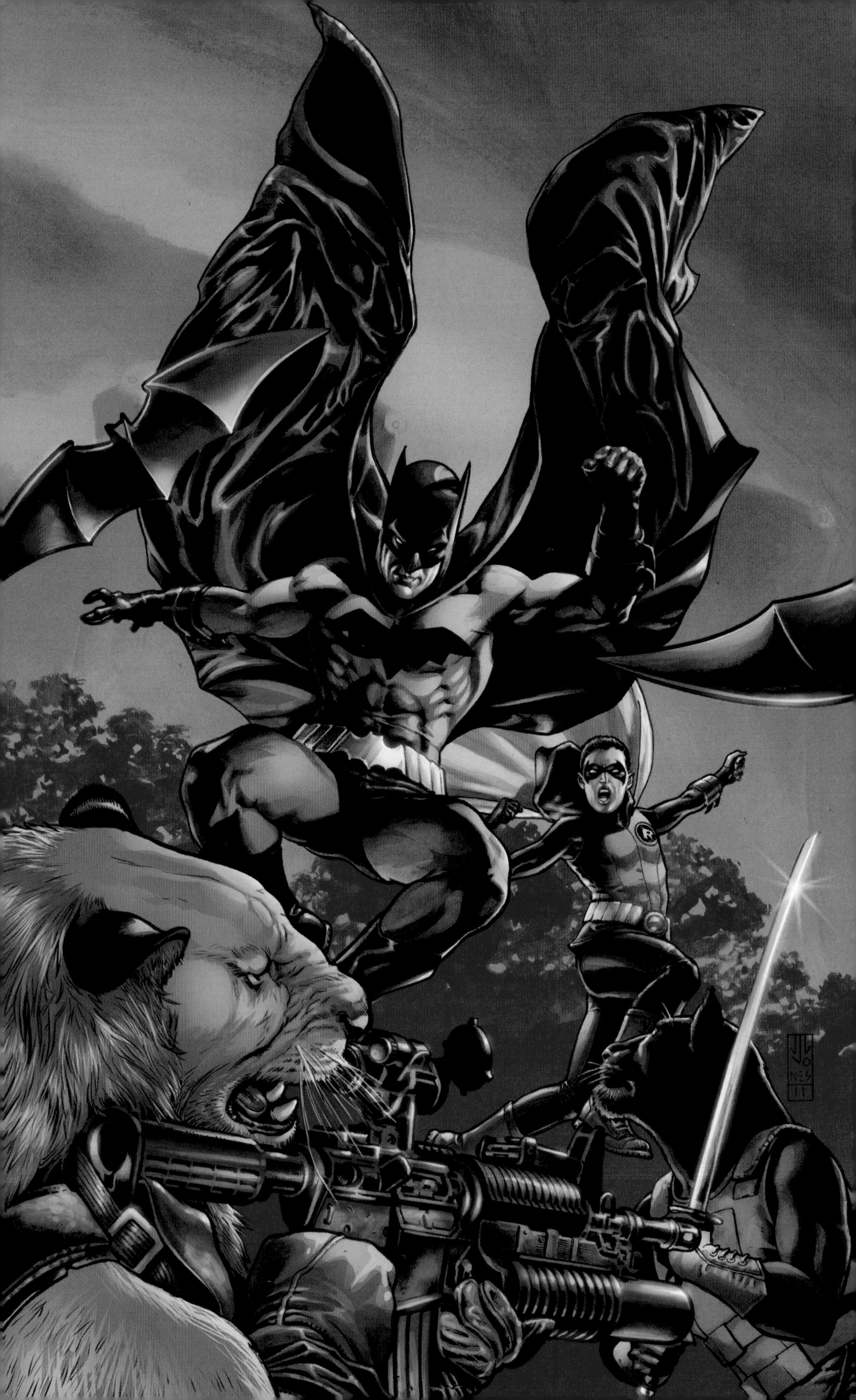

LONG AGO...

AN INVESTIGATIVE MIND AND PHYSICAL SKILLS ARE JUST *TOOLS.*

THE MOST IMPORTANT WEAPON IN YOUR ARSENAL WILL BE YOUR ABILITY TO *ADAPT.*

WE CAN STUDY, WE CAN CONDITION, WE CAN PLAN, BUT *MOST* OF WHAT WE DO IS DEAL WITH CHALLENGES AND OBSTACLES WITH *NO* PRIOR WARNING.

WE PREPARE FOR THE UNKNOWABLE AND WHEN FACED WITH THEM--THINK QUICKLY AND ACT *QUICKER.*

I HEAR YOU. WHEN WE'RE IN A BIND, DON'T *PANIC.*

NO.

IT'S MUCH MORE THAN "NOT PANICKING." STAYING COOL IS A GIVEN. THAT'S THE *LEAST* OF WHAT I EXPECT FROM YOU, JASON.

WHEN YOU'RE AT AN UTTER LOSS AS TO WHAT'S GOING ON AND WHAT WILL HAPPEN NEXT, YOU STEP UP TO THE SITUATION--

"--AND TAKE CONTROL."

YOU GUYS ARE CALLED THE *MENAGERIE*, RIGHT? I THOUGHT YOU WORKED OUT OF SOUTH AMERICA.

USUALLY. BUT TONIGHT WE ARE YOUR *EXTRACTION* TEAM.

YEAH, I SORT OF PIECED THAT PART TOGETHER MYSELF, BUT WHO DO I OWE MY *THANKS* TO FOR SPRINGING ME FROM PRISON?

WE'RE NOT AT LIBERTY TO SAY.

THE STREETS RUN RED
PART 2 OF 3
EXIT STRATEGY

JUDD WINICK WRITER   GREG TOCCHINI ARTIST
ARTUR FUJITA COLORS   PATRICK BROSSEAU LETTERS
COVER BY GUILLEM MARCH   VARIANT COVER BY JG JONES WITH ALEX SINCLAIR

"WE'RE NOT AT LIBERTY TO SAY." YEAH. THAT'S ONE OF THOSE CLICHÉS THAT *NEVER* DOES ANYBODY ANY GOOD. AND IT SETS THE WRONG *TONE.*

LOOK, I DON'T THINK I'M BEING UNREASONABLE HERE, I JUST WANT *SOME* IDEA OF WHAT'S UP.

YOU ARE IN NO DANGER. WE ARE HERE *SIMPLY* TO PROVIDE YOU TRANSPORT. BUT WE ARE UNDER ORDERS NOT TO DISCUSS ANYTHING FURTHER THAN THAT.

WELL, OKAY, I UNDERSTAND. YOU'VE GOT A GIG, YOU'VE GOT TO DO AS THE *BOSS* TELLS YOU.

YOUR COOPERATION IS APPRECIATED.

DON'T SWEAT IT. I *GET* IT. BUT CAN YOU DO ME A SOLID AND LOSE THESE *CUFFS?* THE GUARDS CLIPPED THEM PRETTY TIGHT AND I'M CHAFING.

I AM SORRY, BUT WE'LL HAVE TO--

KUNK!

Not a lot of time.

Got to make every move count.

BLAM!

KA-CHUNG

Good. Got lucky.

They've each got the strength and dexterity of their furry counterparts.

And there's four of them.

CRACK-ACK-ACK-ACK-ACK

Got to get clear of here. Got to get to a ride. I'll never out-run them on foot.

And wherever the hell they're trying to take me--

--I know I don't want to go.

Okay. That takes them down to three.

Crap.

Didn't even hear her comin'--

CRACK!

Ow.

This is going south on me--

--and fast.

Fine!

CRACK ACK-ACK ACK-ACK ACK-ACK ACK-ACK

I'm better off just gunning them all down. Just need to get my shots off without--

CRACK

ALL RIGHT. IT'S TIME TO SETTLE DOWN.

IF YOU DIDN'T NOTICE THE *WOODEN SHEATHS* ON THE SWORDS THAT *PANTHER* IS SWINGING, OR THE *RUBBER BULLETS* COMING FROM *REX'S* RIFLE, LET ME MAKE IT CLEAR--

--WE ARE *SUPPOSED* TO BRING YOU IN *ALIVE.*

DON'T MAKE IT ANY--

THINK!

FINE. ALIVE. BUT BROKEN!

FWIP!

I DON'T THINK SO.

HE'S LEAVING HERE.

BUT HE'S COMING WITH *US.*

WHAT ARE YOU GUYS DOING OUT OF *SOUTH AMERICA?*

THANK GOD. IT'S *BATMAN AND ROBIN.*

LIVE AMMO. REAL *STEEL*.

GO.

THWIP

HIT THEM AND--!

DON'T LET *HIM* GET AWAY! I *KNOW*!

Okay. This wasn't *entirely* unexpected.

THUD

THUD THUD THUD

I knew they'd show up.

But I didn't expect us to be fighting on the *same* side.

I *do* like me some irony.

GOD! YOU'RE HALF *FELINE!* HOW COULD YOU BE SO SLOW?!

BECAUSE SHE WAS SIMPLY *DISTRACTING* YOU.

NOT JUST HER.

YOU'RE VULNERABLE, RED HOOD. NO ARMOR--NO WEAPONS.

CLEP!

JUST SKIN.

AND SKIN DOES SOMETHING TO US ANIMALS!

SPLAA-ARCH!

Funny. I'd thought that Dick would have hit *me* with the *first* adhesive grenade.

That *second* one is coming at me. But a bit too late.

That's the thing with these guys...

...they're always afraid of making the *tough* moves.

It all comes back to Bruce.

That line in the sand.

It limits your options.

I don't have limits.

BLAM

AAAARGH!

HE'S GOT A--!

YES. HE DOES.

I DON'T KNOW IF THE *REPTILE* HERE CAN *REGENERATE,* BUT IF *NOT,* HE'S ONLY GOING TO NEED *ONE* SHOE FROM NOW ON.

BUT I DON'T THINK HE CAN GROW BACK A *HEAD,* SO--

WE CAN TAKE HIM.

DON'T MOVE.

HE'S RIGHT, SHORTY. I'LL *KILL* THIS MURDER-FOR-HIRE DIRTBAG BEFORE YOU COULD TAKE HALF A STEP.

NOW... I'M GOING TO WALK *DINO* HERE, AND IF EITHER OF YOU--

WAIT...

...DON'T... DON'T LEAVE...

...YOU HAVE A CALL.

WELL, HELLO, *BIG RED.* YOU SEEM TO HAVE SCREWED THINGS UP FOR US TONIGHT, HUH?

WHO THE HELL IS--

I MEAN *ALL* WE WANTED TO DO WAS BREAK YOU OUT OF THE POKEY. WE DIDN'T EXPECT A *HUG* OR ANYTHING, BUT GETTING IN BED WITH *BATMAN* AND BEATING THE SPIT OUT OF MY *ZOO CREW,* THAT'S JUST RUDE.

NICE TALKING WITH YOU.

JUST HANG ON THERE, BAD BOY. WE'RE NOT NEARLY DONE.

YOU ARE GOING TO COME IN. HANDS IN THE *AIR.* GIVE YOURSELF UP.

IT'S *THAT...*

...OR WE'RE GOING TO *WHACK* HER.

WHO?

THE ONLY ONE *YOU* SEEM TO GIVE A RAT'S ASS ABOUT.

I THINK YOU CALL HER *SCARLET.*

THIS *SUCKS.*

I'M ODDLY PROUD THAT YOU ARE *FINALLY* UTILIZING YOUTHFUL COLLOQUIALISMS.

ARE YOU *LISTENING* TO ME? IT'S *IDIOTIC.*

I *AM* LISTENING AND YOUR OBJECTION HAS BEEN NOTED.

I DON'T WANT IT TO BE *NOTED*, I WANT YOU TO GET YOUR HEAD IN THE GAME AND REALIZE HOW *UTTERLY* MORONIC THIS IS.

IT HAS ITS RISKS, BUT THIS IS THE *ONLY* PLAY.

NO. THE *OTHER* "PLAY" IS THAT WE BEAT HIM DOWN AND DRAG HIM BACK TO A CONCRETE ROOM. *WHERE HE BELONGS.*

SCARLET'S IN TROUBLE.

SHE'S *BAIT.*

HENCE THE TROUBLE SHE'S IN.

IT'S A *TRAP.*

NO. A *TRAP* WOULD HAVE AN ELEMENT OF *SURPRISE.* THIS IS ALL PRETTY STRAIGHT-FORWARD. JASON TURNS HIMSELF OVER, SHE GOES FREE.

WE *SHOULD* DROP HIM, *SHACKLED*, ON THEIR STOOP AND TAKE THE GIRL. THEN PUT HER IN A JUVENILE DETENTION CENTER.

THAT'S NOT THE PLAY. WE'RE GOING TO RESCUE HER.

AND HERE WE ARE AT HIS *SECRET ARSENAL*? DOESN'T IT BOTHER YOU THAT HE MANAGED TO SLIP BY US, THAT HE HAD A *STASH* OF WEAPONS AND TECH OUT HERE?

ACTUALLY *THAT* BOTHERS ME QUITE A BIT. BUT HE WON'T COME WILLINGLY IF HE'S *UNARMED.*

WHAT HAPPENS WHEN HE DECIDES TO TURN HIS GUNS ON *US?*

DAMIAN, SITUATIONS PRESENT THEMSELVES AND ONE OF OUR GREATEST ABILITIES HAS TO BE *ADAPTATION.*

I'D RATHER HAVE A *PLAN.*

I WOULD, TOO. BUT JASON CAN HEAR US.

HE CAN?

HE'S GOT THE BUILDING WIRED.

HE'S RIGHT ABOUT THAT, DAMIAN. AND I'M SORRY THAT THIS GIG IS MAKING YOU *UNCOMFORTABLE.*

YOU SURE?

IT'S WHAT *I* WOULD HAVE DONE.

BUT SOMETIMES YOU'VE GOT TO LIE DOWN WITH DOGS.

"AND YOU WAKE UP WITH FLEAS."

KID, IF YOU DON'T THINK YOU'RE NOT "WAKING UP WITH FLEAS" *ALREADY,* THEN YOU JUST AREN'T PAYING ATTENTION.

THANKS FOR LETTING ME GET DRESSED. I HAD TO PULL TOGETHER SOMETHING WITH A FEW SPARES...

...BUT I THINK IT'LL WORK.

THIS SUCKS.

NOBODY KNOWS THAT MORE THAN ME.

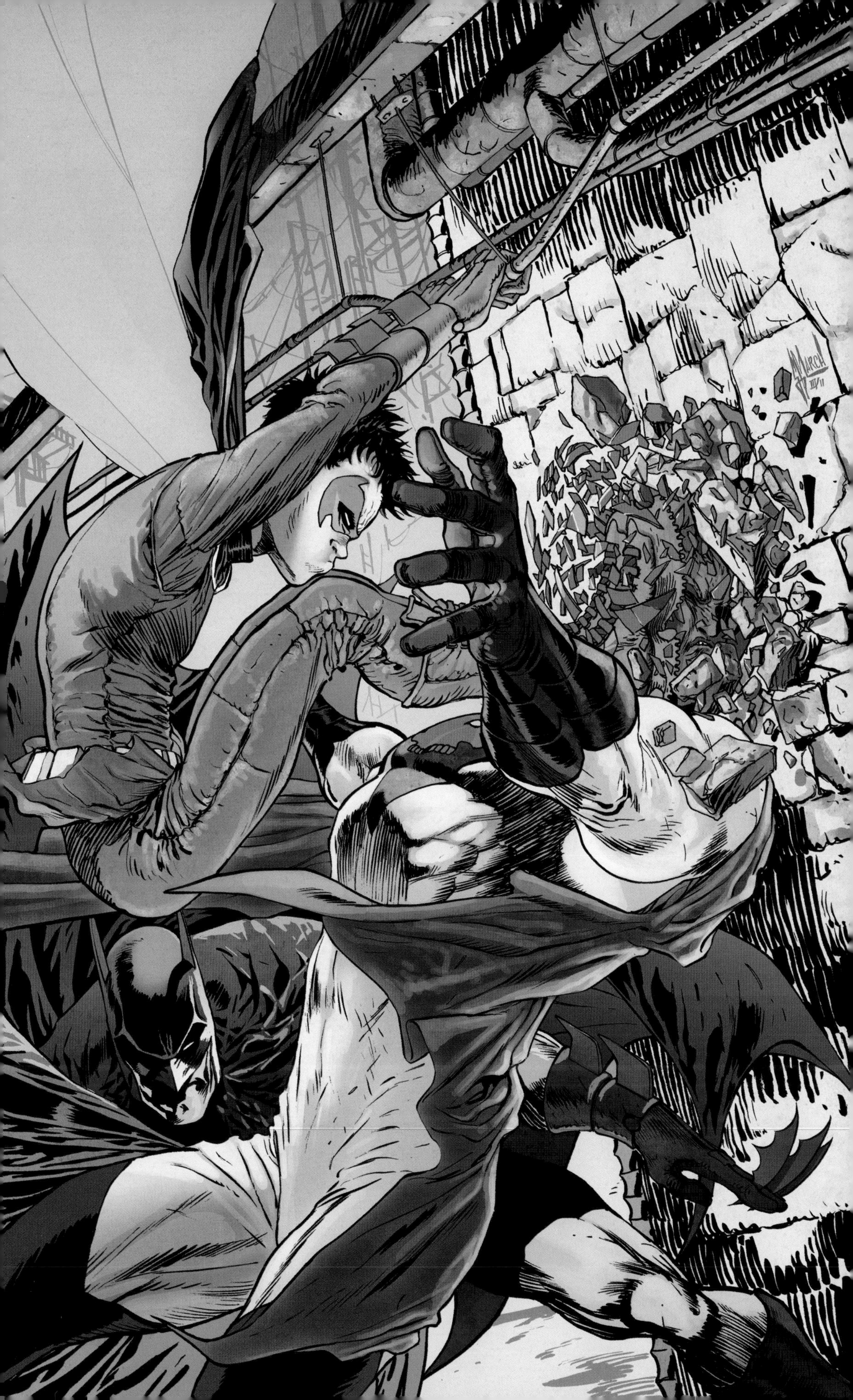
MARCH
III/11

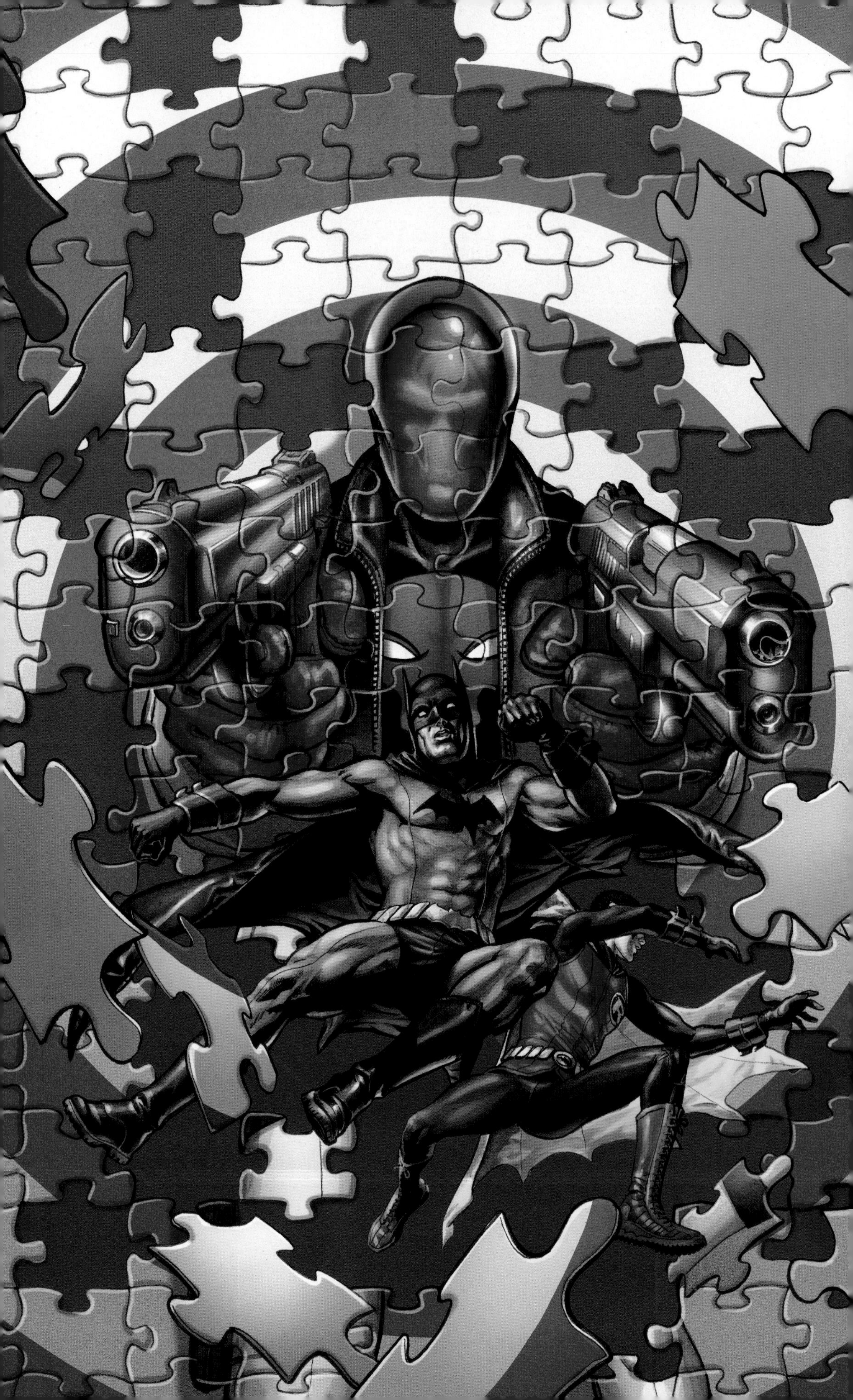

Her name is *Sasha*.

HE'S GOING TO *KILL* YOU.

Her father was murdered in front of her by **Professor Pyg,** and she was scared.

Both inside and out.

NO, HE'S *NOT.* HE DOESN'T WANT ANYTHING TO HAPPEN TO *YOU.* THAT'S WHY WE GRABBED YOU.

But the **Red Hood** found her.

HE'LL RESCUE ME AND *THEN* HE'LL KILL YOU.

THAT'S SWEET. YOU'VE GOT THIS WHOLE *AVENGING ANGEL* THING GOING ON WITH HIM. SOUNDS LIKE *FATHER ISSUES.*

And she became *Scarlet.*

YOU'RE *VERY* STUPID.

She was someone to fight by his side.

I'M A *LOT* OF THINGS, SWEETIE. *STUPID* ISN'T ONE OF THEM.

A familiar and complicated relationship.

HE KILLS PEOPLE WHO DO *WRONG.* LIKE *YOU.* AND YOU WERE STUPID ENOUGH TO TELL HIM WHERE YOU ARE.

"*JASON TODD* IS COMING FOR YOU."

WHAT IS THAT SMELL? *PINE?* YOU ACTUALLY LET ALFRED CLEAN UP THE VEHICLES' INTERIORS WITH *SCENTED* CLEANSERS?

BRUCE WOULD *NEVER* LET HIM DO THAT.

THE STREETS RUN RED
PART 3 OF 3
BOYS' NIGHT OUT

JUDD WINICK WRITER GREG TOCCHINI ARTIST PGS 1-16 ANDY SMITH ARTIST PGS 17-20
ARTUR FUJITA COLORS PATRICK BROSSEAU LETTERS COVER BY GUILLEM MARCH
VARIANT COVER BY JG JONES WITH ALEX SINCLAIR

HE ALWAYS SAID HE NEVER WANTED HIS *OLFACTORY* SENSES MUDDLED WITH THIS CRAP.

I THINK HE JUST DIDN'T LIKE THE BATMOBILE SMELLING *NICE*.

"NICE" AND *BATMAN* DON'T REALLY GEL, DO THEY?

BUT HERE WE ARE. *YOU'RE* BATMAN IN YOUR HOVERCRAFT, STINKING LIKE *CHRISTMAS*.

I GUESS DICK GRAYSON IS THE *NICE* BATMAN.

YOUR INANE JABBERING *WON'T* WORK.

THIS THINLY VEILED ATTEMPT TO BE BOTH FAMILIAR *AND* PASSIVE AGGRESSIVE WILL NEITHER DISARM *NOR* UNBALANCE US.

WOW. THIS IS ONE TIGHT-ASSED SIDEKICK. NOT A LOT OF *QUIPS* GONNA BE COMING OUT OF *THIS ROBIN*, HUH, DICK?

MAYBE *PUBERTY* WILL LOOSEN HIM UP. THOSE HORMONES TEND TO LET THE MIND *WANDER* A BIT MORE.

IF HE LIVES THAT LONG.

SHUT UP.

THIS IS REQUIRING RESTRAINT FROM *ALL* OF US. THE *LEAST* YOU CAN DO IS--

WHAT?

NOT ACT LIKE A *TOOL*.

FINE, WHATEVER.

IT WAS WORTH IT JUST TO HEAR SOMEONE SAY *"TOOL"* WHILE WEARING THE COWL.

BUT I SHOULD GO.

BLAM

I'VE GOT EYES ON HIM! HE'S OUT OF THE BATMOBILE!

ARE BATMAN AND ROBIN IN PURSUIT?!

YES! BUT I DON'T THINK THEY'LL CATCH HIM!

HE'S GOT TOO GOOD A LEAD.

CAN YOU FOLLOW HIM WITHOUT BATMAN SPOTTING YOU?! I WANT TO MAINTAIN A VISUAL AS LONG--

HANG ON. THIS IS HIM.

WHY *HELLO*, MR. TODD.

I'M FLYING *SOLO* NOW. WHERE DO YOU WANT TO DO THIS?

NO PLACE SPECIAL.

"BUT SINCE IT'S A SCHOOL NIGHT AND ALL..."

They usually reserve naming schools for dead presidents.

But in Gotham, *Thomas Wayne* is a dead president.

THOMAS WAYNE MIDDLE SCHOOL

I actually went here for three months.

It sucks to be here *now* as much as it did then.

SEND HER OUT AND I'LL COME IN!

PLEASE. LET'S PRETEND WE'RE NOT *ALL* BRAIN DEAD.

TOSS THE GUNS. AND STRIP.

FINE BY ME.

I GOTTA SAY... I'M FEELING A BIT *VIOLATED*...

...AND THIS COMING FROM A DUDE WHO JUST STEPPED OUT OF *PRISON.*

WE'RE *SLIGHTLY* MORE HIGH-TECH HERE, TODD. NO ANKLE GRABBING AND RUBBER GLOVES.

YOU SAY THAT LIKE IT'S A *GOOD* THING.

JUST HOLD STILL FOR THE SCANS.

NO FOREIGN BODIES. HE'S CLEAN.

GREAT. OFF YOU GO. FLY, BE FREE.

JASON! DON'T DO THIS!

IT'S FINE, KID. JUST GO. WALK *AWAY* FROM THE VERY OBNOXIOUS WOMAN.

NO! WHAT'S GOING TO HAPPEN TO *YOU?!*

WHY IS THE *WIND* PICKING UP...?

NO IDEA, SCARLET. BUT IF THEY WANTED TO KILL ME, I'D BE DEAD ALREADY.

I'M NAKED AND COLD. SO, *PLEASE* JUST GET CLEAR OF THE BUILDING. *NOW.*

IS IT?

THAT *MIGHT* BE THE STEALTH *AIRSHIP* OVERHEAD!

HOW THE HELL DID THEY *FIND US?!*

THEY TRACKED ME FROM THE G.P.S. I *SWALLOWED* THAT DIDN'T SHOW UP ON YOUR SCANS.

BLAM BLAM BLAM

DON'T MOVE. I'VE GOT YOU.

NO.

WE HAVE HER.

And *now* it all gets very interesting.

When life shoots you out of a cannon, you know what you need to do?

Land.

STOP. YOU WON'T KILL ANYONE. NOT HERE.

NOT WITH ME.

CAN WE JUST GET THE GIRL, "BATMAN," AND WORRY ABOUT THE SAFETY OF MURDEROUS ASSASSINS LATER?!

NO ONE DIES!

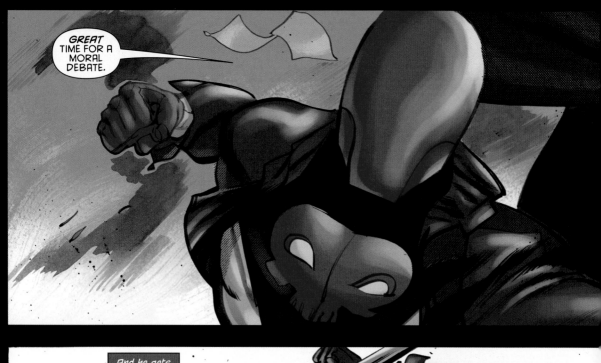

GREAT TIME FOR A MORAL DEBATE.

And he gets angry. *Really* angry.

That anger, it'd make him a great Batman, if he'd let it.

He's trying too much to be like *him*.

The good son.

JUST SHUT UP AND FIGHT.

Dick is different from Bruce. In the way he fights. In the way he thinks.

And the way he feels.

But he won't.

Man, I hate him.

CAN'T SEE HER! WHERE IS--

THERE!

GOT HER!

HANG TIGHT--WE'RE HEADING FOR OUR RIDE.

NO.

BLAM

Not your ride.

CHHU-UNNK

DON'T WORRY--

--I HAVE YOU.

TELL ME QUICK--HOW DID THEY GET YOU HERE?!

I WAS DRUGGED, BUT I THOUGHT I HEARD ROTORS! I THINK THEY'VE GOT--

OUR RIDE.

He won't try to get to us on foot. He knows I have enough of a lead on him.

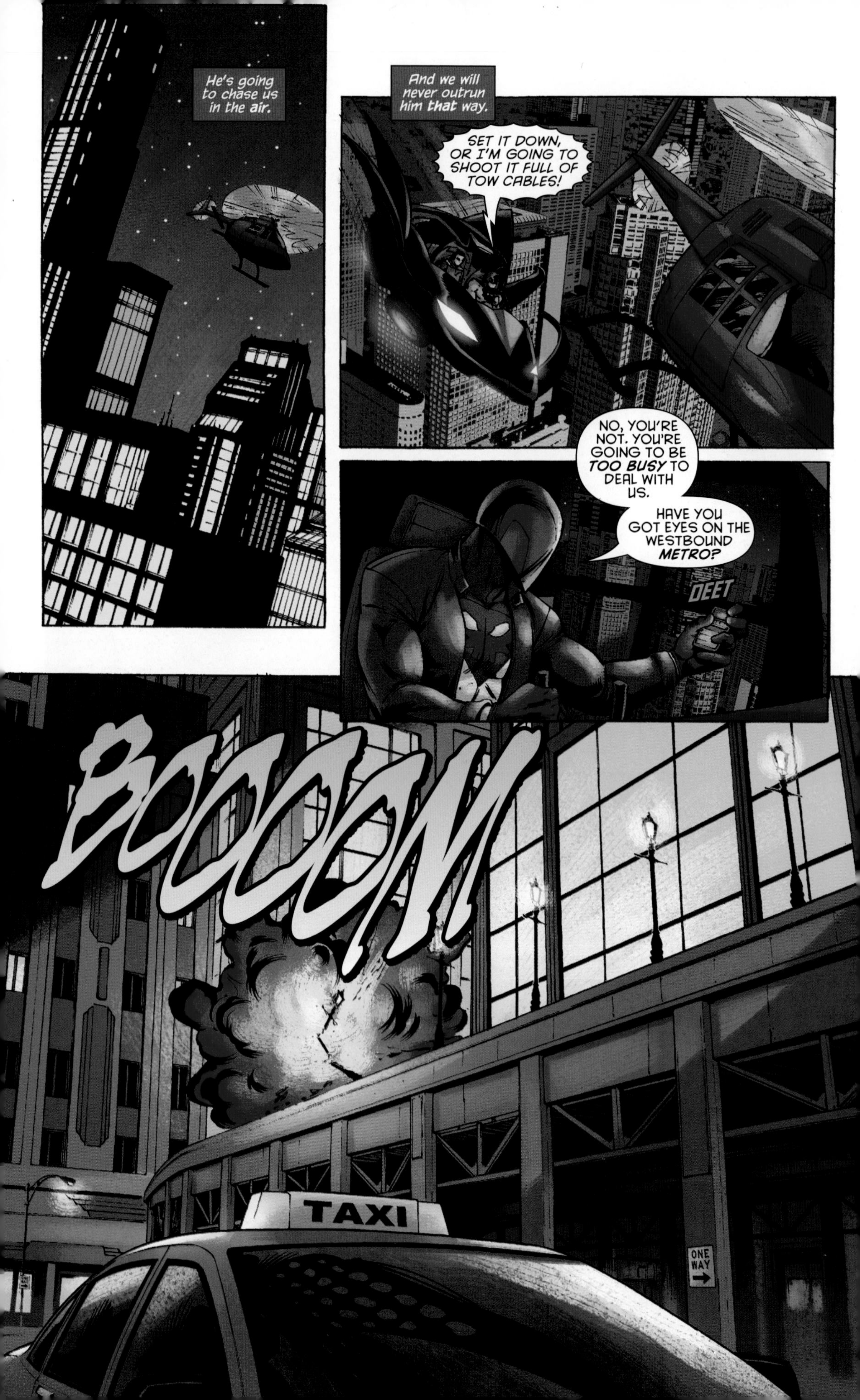
He's going to chase us in the air.
And we will never outrun him that way.
SET IT DOWN, OR I'M GOING TO SHOOT IT FULL OF TOW CABLES!
NO, YOU'RE NOT. YOU'RE GOING TO BE TOO BUSY TO DEAL WITH US.
HAVE YOU GOT EYES ON THE WESTBOUND METRO?
DEET
BOOOOM
TAXI
ONE WAY

THERE ARE *SIX* MORE OF THOSE EXPLOSIVES ALL ALONG THE RAIL LINE! YOU COULD DEFUSE THEM OR *CHASE US!*

HOW DID HE PLANT BOMBS ON--?!

MUST HAVE DONE IT *MONTHS* AGO.

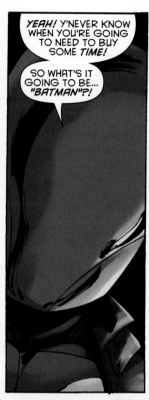

YEAH! Y'NEVER KNOW WHEN YOU'RE GOING TO NEED TO BUY SOME *TIME!*

SO WHAT'S IT GOING TO BE... *"BATMAN"?!*

ME OR THE *DEATHS* OF A FEW HUNDRED PEOPLE?

CALL THE BOMB SQUAD! OR GET THEM TO SHUT DOWN THE TRAINS!

HE'S MONITORING THE POLICE BAND. HE'D KNOW.

WE ARE *NOT* GOING TO JUST LET HIM--

YES, WE ARE.

THIS *SUCKS!*

NO ONE KNOWS IT MORE THAN ME.

YOU OKAY, SASHA?

I'M GOOD. *THANK YOU.*

IT'S FINE. YOU WANT ME TO DROP YOU SOMEWHERE?

I WANT... I WANT TO STAY WITH YOU.

WORKS FOR ME.

WHERE ARE WE GOING?

DON'T KNOW YET.

BUT THAT'S NEVER STOPPED ME BEFORE.

THE END

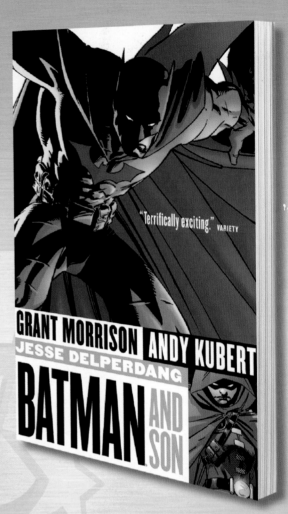
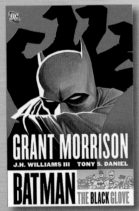